OLD TESTAMENT LEGENDS

T0371370

OLD TESTAMENT LEGENDS

*FROM A GREEK POEM ON
GENESIS AND EXODUS By*
GEORGIOS CHUMNOS

*Edited with Introduction, Metrical
Translation, Notes & Glossary from
a Manuscript in the British Museum*

By

F. H. MARSHALL, M.A.
Birkbeck College; Reader in Classics, University of London

CAMBRIDGE
AT THE UNIVERSITY PRESS
1925

CAMBRIDGE
UNIVERSITY PRESS

University Printing House, Cambridge CB2 8BS, United Kingdom

Cambridge University Press is part of the University of Cambridge.

It furthers the University's mission by disseminating knowledge in the pursuit of
education, learning and research at the highest international levels of excellence.

www.cambridge.org
Information on this title: www.cambridge.org/9781316509630

© Cambridge University Press 1925

This publication is in copyright. Subject to statutory exception
and to the provisions of relevant collective licensing agreements,
no reproduction of any part may take place without the written
permission of Cambridge University Press.

First published 1925
First paperback edition 2015

A catalogue record for this publication is available from the British Library

ISBN 978-1-316-50963-0 Paperback

Cambridge University Press has no responsibility for the persistence or accuracy
of URLs for external or third-party internet websites referred to in this publication,
and does not guarantee that any content on such websites is, or will remain,
accurate or appropriate.

PREFACE

THIS selection from the hitherto unpublished poem of Georgios Chumnos on Genesis and Exodus comprises a little more than a fourth of the whole work. It is printed with a twofold hope. On the one hand it is possible that the legends, which played so important a part in the religious education of the masses in Mediaeval Europe, may be found of interest and instruction even in the present day, and such interest may be enhanced by the small selection from the wealth of coloured illustrations with which the British Museum manuscript is decorated. On the other hand it is hoped that these extracts from a poem which has never before appeared in print may increase the interest taken in the popular language of Mediaeval Greece. It has too long been the habit of classical scholars to dismiss such Greek as 'barbarous,' apparently on the ground that what they cannot understand must be so regarded. It is surely a matter for some surprise that in the case of a language which has an unbroken history for nearly three thousand years and is a living force at the present day such an attitude should still be maintained. Works such as the present, which are written phonetically and preserve the spoken language of their time, have a distinct value for the history of the Greek language.

The metrical English translation is free, but it is hoped that it does not do violence to the sense of the original in any material point. The Notes and Glossary serve to some extent to supplement it, but until the study of Mediaeval and Modern Greek is more widely pursued in England, it would be idle to treat such a work from a strictly philological standpoint.

I have to express my warm thanks to the Publication Fund of the University of London and to Birkbeck College whose grants have enabled me to publish these selections. Prof. R. M. Dawkins most kindly went through the whole of the Greek text with me and gave me invaluable assistance in interpreting it, but for any errors I am of course solely responsible.

F. H. MARSHALL.

LONDON,
November, 1924.

CONTENTS

LIST OF ILLUSTRATIONS

INTRODUCTION

THE manuscript of the Greek paraphrase of Genesis and Exodus by Georgios Chumnos, from which the present metrical translation has been made, is numbered Add. MS 40724 in the British Museum Collection, and was acquired by purchase in 1922. It was once in the possession of Sir Thomas Brooke. Two other manuscripts of the poem were previously known, viz. those at Vienna and Venice respectively, and these are mentioned by Krumbacher in his *Gesch. der byzantinischen Litteratur* (2nd ed. 1897), p. 818 f. Neither has been edited, though Krumbacher gives the first four lines of the poem as a specimen. From the Vienna MS it appears that Chumnos was a native of the town of Chandax (Candia) in Crete.

The British Museum MS is exceptionally well preserved, written in a large and clear hand on pages of about 25 by 18 cm., with comparatively few abbreviations. The most striking feature, however, is the coloured illustrations inserted in the text in panels. There are no fewer than 375 of these, excellently preserved, and though the drawing is not first-rate, they are full of spirit and never sink into carelessness. They supply a most complete series of illustrations to the parts of Genesis and Exodus dealt with in the poem. The scribe and the artist were evidently the same person, as might be inferred from the manner in which the illustrations are fitted into the body of the text.

This inference is borne out by four rhymed couplets
of rude style appended to the poem in a different
hand, which appear to give much too modest an
estimate of the scribe-artist's work. The following
translation may serve to indicate their spirit:

'With all the care it could command the penman's hand
did write
This ancient book, which doth its tale of history indite.
And yet of all the wondrous deeds that history could
relate
The greater part for lack of space the poet doth not
state.
Although the book be barbarous in letters and in art,
And other faults besides you'll spy in this—the
penman's—part,
Yet surely many a happy rhyme in the poet's work
you'll find,
The product of his artist skill and understanding
mind[1].'

The poem consists of a little over 2800 lines and
occupies with the illustrations 137 folios. The
authorship is claimed in the following lines at the
end:

'Thus these two books that Moses wrote have reached
their destined goal,
Nought that I purposed is unsaid, I have embraced
the whole.

[1] Με κόπον περισσότατον ὑπάρχει γεγραμμένον
τὸ παλαιὸν βιβλόπουλον τοῦτο τὸ στορϊσμένον.
'Αμὴ τὰ περισσότερα δὲν τὰ διαλαμβάνει
θαύμαστα καὶ ἱστορικά, καὶ εἶναι λειψὸν πάνυ.
Καλὰ καὶ εἶναι βάρβαρον στὴν τέχνην τῶν γραμμάτων,
ὁμοίως κεῖς τὴν ζωγραφιὰν καὶ τῶν λοιπῶν πραγμάτων,
'Αμ' ἔπρεπε πολύτεραις ῥήμαις νὰ κατορθώσει
ὁ ποιητὴς με σύνθεσιν καὶ σοφοτέραν γνῶσις.

Georgios Chumnos with due zeal in verses rhymed did
  write;
Of Genesis and Exodus this tale he did indite[1].'

The British Museum MS comes from the monastery of Mount Sinai, as is shown by the following
inscription written at the end of the poem:

αὕτη ἡ βίβλος ὑπάρχει τοῦ ἁγίου ὄρους Σινᾶι, κὶ
εἴ τις τὸ ξενόσει ἐκ τοῦ ἁγίου μοναστηρίου, νὰ ἔχει τὰς
ἀρᾶς τῶν ἁγίων πατέρων· ὁποῦ κόψη τὸ φίλω....

'This book belongs to the Holy Mountain of
Sinai, and if any one takes it from the holy monastery, he will incur the curses of the holy fathers;
if any one cuts a leaf....' This last penalty is con-
cealed in a kind of rebus which I have not been
able to resolve, but it seems likely that 'let him
be excommunicated' is intended.

In addition to this inscription an interesting
cipher is written on the first leaf of the manuscript.
The solution of this is due to Messrs Gilson and
Bell of the Department of Manuscripts in the
British Museum, who have generously placed it
at my disposal. The following is a transcript and
translation:

αχμς Ἰουνίου κ̄. Ἔκαμαν εἰς τὸ Μησύρι οἰκονόμον
τὸν στραβὸν Γιακήμη· καὶ διὰ νὰ μὴν δώση ἕνα ῥέτουλο
τυρὶ καὶ ἕνα ῥέτουλο μέλη, ἐζημίωσαν τὸ μοναστήρι

[1]   Τὰ δυὸ βιυλία τοῦ Μωϋσῆ τόρα ξετελειοθήκα,
         στὸν τόπον αὐτὸν τὸν ἔρχησα τίβοτες δεναφῆκα.
      Γεωργίτζη Χούμνος μὲ σπουδή
         ἐβάλθηκεν νὰ γράψη
      Στὴν Γένεσιν καὶ Ἔξοδον σὲ ῥῆμαν νὰ τὴν
         Τάξιν.

γρόσα χιλιάδες η καὶ ριάλια διακόσ(ι)α. ὅπου νὰ ἔχῃ
τὸ ἀνάθεμα, καὶ ὅποιος ἦτον ἀφορμὴ νὰ τὸν κάμουν
οἰκονόμον· κὲ ἃς δώ(σ)ουν λόγον τῷ Θεῷ ἐν ἡμέρᾳ
κρίσεως.

'Year 1646, June 20. They made the squint-
eyed Yacimi steward at Cairo, and because he did
not give a *rotl* of cheese and a *rotl* of honey, they
fined the monastery 8000 piastres and 200 reals.
May he be accursed, and whoever was the cause
of making him steward. And let them give account
to God in the Day of Judgment[1].'

The meaning apparently is that the Turks fined
the monastery of Sinai, because the steward of the
Sinaitic Μετόχιον at Cairo had refused to give a
small offering to a Turkish official.

CHARACTER OF THE POEM.

The poem, which Krumbacher places at about
1500, was evidently written for the masses rather
than for the learned. This is shown at once by the
language, which is full of popular words and must
approximate to the spoken language of the period
at which it was written, and also by the general
simplicity of the narrative and the wealth of
legendary matter introduced. The choice of epi-
sodes and legends seems expressly designed to
appeal to the popular imagination, though a didactic

---

[1] The original form of the cipher will be found in my article
on the ms in *Byzantinisch-Neugriechische Jahrbücher*, iv. p. 96 ff.,
and an amended transcript and interpretation is given *ibid*.
p. 426 by N. S. Phirippides, who points out that ῥέτουλο =
Arabic *rotl*, a measure of weight.

aim may also be detected[1]. It is not necessary to enter into a detailed and critical discussion of the numerous legends incorporated in the poem, but since these are all-important for a proper understanding of the historical development of this class of composition, it will be best first to give a brief summary of them in the order in which they occur, and then to try to ascertain what information is available as to their origin and distribution.

I. *Bond signed for the Devil by Adam and Eve.* (P. 2.)

When Adam and Eve were expelled from Paradise, they had never experienced darkness. In their terror at its approach they were met by the Devil, who offered to restore to them the light of day on condition that they signed a bond surrendering themselves and their descendants to his power. They signed and discovered the fraud when it was too late.

II. *Adam and Eve instructed by an angel to bury Abel's body.* (P. 6.)

Adam and Eve did not understand what death was, and when Abel's body began to decay they had to be instructed by an angel as to his burial.

III. *Cain shot by the blind Lamech.* (P. 10, Fig. 2.)

Lamech, though blind, was famous as an archer and huntsman. One day, accompanied by his young

---

[1] We have only to compare Chumnos's poem with the anonymous *Story of Genesis and Exodus* in early English—ca. 1250 (edited by R. Morris in the Early English Text Society Series, No. 7)—to see how great is the superiority of Chumnos in point of general interest and poetic style.

son as guide, he heard a rustling in a thick bed of reeds. It was caused by Cain who had taken refuge there and was shaking with the terror of his sin. Lamech, thinking that a wild beast was lurking in the reeds, let fly his arrow and killed Cain. When he knew the truth he was overcome with despair and in his anger killed his son also. But by the mercy of God he was the first to obtain pardon.

IV. *Seth sent by the dying Adam to Paradise to beg for the Oil of Mercy.* (P. 16, Figs. 3–6.)

Adam, racked with pains in the head which foreboded death, sends his son Seth to Paradise to beg for the Oil of Mercy promised by God at the time of his expulsion. Seth after a long journey arrives outside the gate and in trepidation tells his mission to the Archangel. He is bidden to look at the wonders of Paradise. There he sees the tree of knowledge all stripped of its leaves, but amid the high boughs he marks a babe in swaddling bands weeping incessantly. 'That,' says the Archangel, 'is the Son of God weeping for your parents' sin.' In the end Seth is given three seeds which he puts into the mouth of the dead Adam. From these seeds sprout three great branches of pine, cypress and cedar wood respectively, which are united in a single stem.

V. *Enoch inscribes on marble tablets the story of the Creation.* (P. 34, Fig. 7.)

Enoch, foreseeing that fire or flood would overwhelm the wicked giants, took marble tablets and inscribed on them the story of God's marvellous works in order that such record might survive to after time.

VI. *The conversion of Abram.* (P. 36, Figs. 8–10.)
Terah, the father of Abram, was a maker of idols, and his son used to carry the images to market. It fell out that Abram through contemplation of the wondrous works of heaven was seized with a longing to know their Creator and His ways, and God in His mercy sent an angel who revealed the truth. The angel told Abram that he must depart from his home and seek out a new land in which his seed was destined to grow and multiply. Abram returned home and told Terah all that had happened, and Terah embraced with joy the revelation of the true God. He and all his family leave their home and set out for Mesopotamia.

VII. *Abraham, Sarah and the king of Canaan.* (P. 44, Figs. 11–13.)
When Abraham arrived in Canaan he feared that Sarah's beauty might lead to his destruction, so they agreed that she should be called his sister. The king of Canaan ordered that Sarah should be led to his couch, but when he endeavoured to approach her, he was threatened by an angel with drawn sword. In his terror he besought Abraham to tell the whole truth. Abraham told him that Sarah was his wife and that God had promised him the land of Canaan for himself and his descendants. The king yielded up the land, and left Abraham rich presents of flocks and herds.

VIII. *The story of Melchisedek.* (P. 56, Figs. 14–17.)

God gave Abraham command to set out on a journey and to seek out a cave in the Northern mountain-face. There he would find a strange dweller—a wild man whose nails exceeded a cubit in length, whose hair and beard fell to his feet and whose body was shaggier than a sheep's. This man he must shear and clothe. Abraham duly obeyed, and found out the man who was Melchisedek. He told him God's command, and Melchisedek received him kindly and suffered himself to·be shorn and clothed, and then told his strange story. He was the son of Iasedek, a king devoted to idol-worship. One day his father ordered him to fetch sheep in order that he might do sacrifice to his heathen gods, but as Melchisedek went upon his way he was brought through contemplation of the wonders of the heavens to a knowledge of the true God. He straightway returned home and besought his father to give up his idols. His father was seized with passion and declared that he would offer up Melchisedek himself as a sacrifice together with his subjects' children. Again he was sent to fetch sheep for this sacrifice, but meanwhile his mother sent out his brother to warn him to escape. He fled to this mount which he called Olivet and prayed God to send down doom upon the idolaters. His prayer was answered, and he saw all the city and its inhabitants overthrown by earthquake. In terror at the sight he took refuge in the cave where he had remained unvisited by human face for forty

years. Melchisedek offered sacrifice to God out of
the stores which Abraham had brought, and then
the two ate and drank. Abraham returned home,
and out of gratitude to God promised Him the
tithe of all that he possessed.

IX. *Abraham and the three young travellers.*
(P. 72, Figs. 18, 19.)
Though the story of Abraham's entertainment
of the three young travellers (typifying the Holy
Trinity) follows in the main that narrated in the
Bible, there are two legends introduced into it,
viz. the activity of the Devil, who did his best to
keep the wayfarers from Abraham's hospitable
door, and the story of the resurrection of the calf
slain by Abraham for the entertainment of his
guests.

X. *The assault upon Lot's house.* (P. 78, Figs.
20, 21.)
The difference from the Biblical story consists
in the driving back of the assailants by a sheet
of flame launched from the doorway, instead of
the blinding mentioned in the Bible. Moreover
the three travellers are not in Chumnos's version
reduced to two.

XI. *The purification of Lot.* (P. 84, Figs. 22, 23.)
Lot, after he had been made drunk and had
committed incest with his two daughters, told
Abraham what had happened. Abraham was sorely
grieved at the sin and told Lot that he must go to
the Nile and fetch thence three brands of wood, if
perchance he might win pardon and purification

from God. Abraham never thought that Lot would return safe from his adventurous journey, but, under the guidance of God's hand, he brought back the three brands of cedar, pine and cypress. These they planted in the form of a triangle on the side of a barren hill. Next Lot was told to go and fetch water from the Jordan to pour upon the brands which at last burst into blossom. These brands which blossomed signify redemption for man's sins.

XIII. *Pharaoh and the infant Moses.* (P. 100, Figs. 26, 27.)

The princess brought the child Moses at the age of four years to her father who welcomed the boy kindly and took him into his arms. The child stretched out his hands and tore Pharaoh's beard. The king in his rage ordered Moses to be removed and put to death, but the Princess pleaded for him and begged that there might be a test to prove that his deed was simply due to a child's thoughtlessness. Pharaoh ordered that two similar bowls should be brought—one containing fire, the other coins lighted up by the fire—and set before the child. Moses stretched out his hands and seized the fire which he put to his lips. His bitter cry of pain satisfied the king that the child was innocent, and so his life was spared.

XIV. *The death of Moses.* (P. 106, Fig. 28.)

Moses gave command, and they dug a grave for him upon Sinai. He entered the grave as though to make trial of it, but God sent down a mist which covered the grave and he was seen no more.

In addition to these main legends there are also numerous small variations from the Biblical text, such as the placing of Adam and Eve's home in a cave called Nevron after their expulsion from Paradise (p. 6, Fig. 1); the throwing of Isaac by Ishmael (instead of the mocking); the naming (Andreas) of the servant sent to fetch a wife for Isaac; the making of Rachel the elder instead of the younger sister; the making of Maria (Miriam) the aunt instead of the sister of Moses (p. 102). Other variations are clearly designed to add picturesqueness to the narrative and nothing more. I give (XII) the episode of the sale of Joseph to the Ishmaelites and his throwing himself on Rachel's tomb on the way to Egypt as an example. (P. 92, Figs. 24, 25.)

The way is now prepared for the consideration of the origin of these legends which Chumnos used so freely. There are two works which I have found specially useful in dealing with this question, viz. A. A. Vassiliev, *Anecdota Graeco-Byzantina*, Moscow, 1893, and V. Jagič, *Slavische Beiträge zu den biblischen Apocryphen* in *Denkschriften der k. Akademie der Wissenschaften*, Wien, 1893. From a study of these works two main facts seem to emerge, viz. that there are two great cycles of legends upon which Chumnos could draw—those connected with Adam and his death and those dealing with the subsequent Biblical history.

Although the light thrown upon the legends by

Vassiliev's work chiefly concerns the later cycle, I will consider it first, because his Introduction is valuable for Chumnos's work as a whole and either the manuscript which he publishes was the chief source for a great part of the present poem, or else both drew freely on a common source.

The manuscript in question is at Vienna (Cod. Vind. theo. 210) and is entitled 'Old Testament History from Adam.' The manuscript itself is of the sixteenth century (the probable date of the Chumnos MS), but Vassiliev shows in his Introduction that the work itself probably dates from the ninth century. Vassiliev also shows that the work is largely based on an earlier book—the *Palaea Interpretata* or 'The Old Testament Interpreted,' which, though originally written in Greek, is only preserved in a Slavonic translation[1]. This latter work, which is of a polemic character, went down to the reign of Solomon, and was intended as a refutation of the Jews and Mohammedans.

The *Palaea Interpretata* laid chief stress on interpreting the Old Testament from the Christian standpoint, but the arguments used were too subtle for the popular intelligence. Hence it came about that in course of time works of a simpler character were produced, such as the *Palaea Historica* we are dealing with, which omitted the theological argu-

---

[1] In an article entitled 'Old Testament Interpretation in Mediaeval Greek and Slavonic Literature' published in the *Church Quarterly Review*, Oct. 1923, pp. 71–85, I have endeavoured to show that large portions of the Greek original are preserved in an unpublished MS in the British Museum.

ments and confined themselves to Biblical narrative interspersed with legends. The result, when accompanied freely by illustrations, was a work corresponding closely to the 'Poor Men's Bibles' much in vogue in Western Europe in the fourteenth to the sixteenth centuries. In fact Chumnos's work is such a Bible, though intended for eastern and not for western readers.

The correspondence of the Vienna *Palaea Historica* with Chumnos's poem is remarkably close as regards both choice of legend and order of arrangement. As regards style and interest, however, there can be no doubt that Chumnos is infinitely superior. He is of course unequal, but I think that he shows considerable skill in extracting what is likely to interest the ordinary reader and often displays no mean power of narration and poetic feeling.

I now give a brief summary of the correspondences of the *Palaea Historica* and Chumnos as regards the legends, following the order of the legends as numbered above. V. followed by a number indicates the page of Vassiliev's work referred to.

(1) Not in Vassiliev.
(2) V. 195. Practically identical.
(3) V. 193 ff. Practically identical[1].
(4) Not in Vassiliev.
(5) V. 196 f. Practically identical. This story of an engraved record of the Creation seems to go back at least in essence to a very early period.

---

[1] Cf. James, *The lost Apocrypha of the O.T.*, p. 10 f.

Josephus (*Ant. Jud.* 1. ii. 3) has the following (Whiston's translation):

'The children of Seth...that their inventions might not be lost before they were sufficiently known, upon Adam's prediction that the world was to be destroyed at one time by force of fire, and at another time by the violence and quantity of water, made two pillars, the one of brick, the other of stone: they inscribed their discoveries on them both, that in case the pillar of brick should be destroyed by the flood, the pillar of stone might remain and exhibit those discoveries to mankind, and also inform them that there was another pillar of brick erected by them.'

(6) V. 201 ff. Practically identical, but some further details are given in Vassiliev. Thus Abram sets fire to the idols, and Atastas, the father of Lot, is burnt in defending them[1].

(7) V. 204 f. Practically identical. The king of Canaan is called E(m)phron son of Hettaios, or simply 'the Hittite.'

(8) V. 206 ff. Practically identical. There are slight variations, *e.g.* V. gives the god to whom Iasedek sacrificed as Cronos. The victim of the sacrifice was determined by lot[2].

(9) V. 214 ff. Mainly as in Chumnos with some slight variations[3].

(10) V. 215 ff. As in Chumnos.

(11) V. 217 f. As in Chumnos. Note corre-

---

[1] Cf. Box, *Apocalypse of Abraham*, pp. viii, 35 ff., 88 ff.

[2] Cf. James, *op. cit.*, p. 17 f.

[3] The resurrection of the calf is mentioned in the *Testament of Abraham*. See James, *Testament of Abraham* (Texts and Studies ed. by J. Armitage Robinson), p. 83, Rec. A, Ch. vi.

spondence in detail, such as the hill where the brands were planted being 24 miles from Jordan[1].

(13) V. 227 f. Here V. differs somewhat. There are two versions; the first makes Moses take Pharaoh's crown and trample it under foot, and then be submitted to the ordeal of fire and gold. The second makes him pluck Pharaoh's beard, and then be submitted to the test of choosing between a gold crown and a naked sword, in which he chooses the sword. In both cases the one who pleads for the child is 'a wise man' and not the princess. The test of fire is given in the early English *Story of Genesis and Exodus* (E.E.T.S. No. 7), ll. 2633 ff.

Here again the main legend goes back to Josephus's time. Cf. *Ant. Jud.* ii. ix. 7 (Whiston's translation):

'And when she (the Princess) had said this, she put the infant into her father's hands: so he took him and hugged him close to his breast, and on his daughter's account, in a pleasant way, put his diadem upon his head. But Moses threw it down to the ground, and in a puerile mood he wreathed it round and trod upon it with his feet; which seemed to bring with it an evil presage concerning the kingdom of Egypt. But when the sacred scribe saw this (he was the same person who foretold that his nativity would bring the dominion of that kingdom low), he made a violent attempt to kill him....But Thermuthis prevented him and snatched the child away. And the king was not hasty to slay him, God Himself, whose providence protected Moses, inclining the king to spare him.'

[1] Both Chumnos and V. have this story in common with Michael Glycas, *Annales*. See Ed. Bekker, ii. p. 135 after the Codex Claromontanus.

Besides these correspondences in the main legends, V. has a number of minor coincidences with Chumnos. Chumnos's story of the raven feasting on the bodies of the giants drowned in the Flood appears in V. 199; Nimrod (called Nevron in Chumnos, p. 36) appears also in V. 201 as the founder of Babylon and the originator of geometry; the number of languages spoken at Babel is in both 72 (V. 201); Abraham's servant is by both named Andreas.

The legend of the death and burial of Moses (14) is quite different in Chumnos (p. 106) and V. 257 f.[1] In V. Moses and Joshua ascend a mountain, and there Moses dies. Joshua informs the people. A contest takes place between the Archangel Michael and one Samuel over the disposal of the body. 'And the Archangel Michael prepared the tomb of Moses in the place where he was ordered by Christ our God and no one saw it.' The burial on Sinai[2] of the Chumnos version fits in curiously with the origin of the present manuscript which was probably written in the monastery on that mountain. It would be interesting to know whether the legend was part of Chumnos's original poem, or whether it is an addition made by the monastery to enhance its prestige. This can only

[1] Cf. James, *The lost Apocrypha of the O.T.*, p. 47 ff.
[2] Dr Rendel Harris in his pamphlet 'A New Christian Apology' (1923), p. 6, draws attention to the fact that in the legend of St Catherine her body is carried away to Mt Sinai, and suggests that, as in the case of Moses, the body was put there in order that it might *not* be found.

be determined by an examination of the Vienna and Venice MSS.

Up to Exodus the general correspondence between Chumnos and V. is very marked. Afterwards the variation becomes more and more noticeable. V. introduces other legends relating to Moses, *e.g.* (p. 228) his fight with the Indians in Pharaoh's service, in the course of which campaign the storks devour serpents which threaten him. In the fight against Amalek V. 237 makes no mention of the supports which are used by Chumnos as symbolic of the Cross. In this part Chumnos tends to be much more compressed than V., and he appears to have relied mainly on the received Biblical version, though he does not hesitate to introduce variations, *e.g.* in the Ten Commandments.

From the above evidence it is difficult to resist the conclusion that Chumnos used the work preserved for us in V.'s MS or at any rate the work from which that MS is derived.

It will have been noticed that two of the principal legends (1 and 4) introduced by Chumnos into the story of Adam and Eve are lacking in V. For these we must turn to the Slavonic MSS.

Jagič in the work above referred to notes nine Slavonic MSS dealing with the Adam and Eve cycle of legends. They range in date from the fifteenth to the eighteenth century, but all apparently go back to a Greek original. Jagič divides them into an earlier group and a later redaction. The earlier redaction bears close relationship to the *Apocalypsis Mosis*, edited in 1866 by C. Tischendorf from four

Greek MSS ranging in date from the eleventh to the fourteenth century. This work is of interest in relation to the Chumnos text chiefly on account of the title: 'Narration and state of Adam and Eve the first-created, revealed by God to his servant Moses, at the time when he received the tables of the law of the Covenant from the Lord's hand, being taught by the Archangel Michael.' Evidently Chumnos is inspired by this idea when in his opening lines he prays to God to enlighten him that he may tell the story of God's words to Moses, the idea being that the whole story of the Creation and subsequent events were revealed by God to Moses. The second redaction of the Slavonic group contains certain additions, notably from the standpoint of the Chumnos MS the legend of the bond signed for the Devil by Adam and Eve (No. 1 above). The Slavonic version, as given by Jagič, p. 9, is as follows:

'Elsewhere in Scripture it is written that Adam was in Paradise praising God together with the archangels and angels, without the light growing dark. At the time he was expelled from Paradise for his sin, he did not know that day and night had previously been ordained by God. He sat with his face towards Paradise, lamenting the loss of the life he had led there, when night came on and it grew dark. And Adam exclaimed, saying: "Woe is me that I neglected Divine law and have been expelled from the splendid life of Paradise, and have lost the light that grew not dark." "O bright light of mine," said he weeping and lamenting, "never shall I see you again nor your splendour which grows not dim nor your fair beauty. Lord, have mercy upon me in my fall!" To him the

Devil came and said: "Why dost thou lament and groan?"
Adam said: "For that splendid light which has hid itself
because of me." The Devil said to him: "I will give you
light, if you bind yourself, your children and your descendants to me by a bond." For the sake of light Adam gave
him a bond and wrote: "O light, to thy possessor I and
my posterity belong." And day came and light shone over
all the earth. But the Devil took the bond and hid it in
Jordan beneath the stone where Christ was baptised[1].'

Another notable addition contained in one of
this second group of MSS is the lament over
Paradise by Adam: 'O Paradise, O Paradise, most
splendid Paradise, Beauty ineffable, created for my
sake, but shut for Eve's offence,' which is also
introduced by Chumnos (p. 2). Jagič notes
(p. 52) that this lament corresponds to the lament
in the liturgy of the Greek Church.

The story of the visit to Paradise to fetch the
Oil of Mercy (Chumnos No. 4 above) is contained
in the *Apocalypsis Mosis*, but the version is very
different from that of Chumnos. The earlier group
of Slavonic MSS brings the story nearer to Chumnos,
but there are still considerable differences. (Jagič,
p. 21 ff.) The story there given is briefly as
follows:

'Adam was racked with sore pains, and bade Eve and
his son Seth to go to Paradise and pray God to give them
of "the tree of oil." On the way they had difficulty in

[1] The germ of this legend occurs in the Ethiopic version of
the *Book of Adam and Eve* (ed. S. C. Malan, p. 15), where the
terror of Adam and Eve at the first dark night is recorded.
This Ethiopic version, which is probably based on an earlier
Arabic version, goes back to the fifth or sixth century after
Christ.

escaping from the jaws of a fearsome wild beast. When
they came to Paradise they saw the Archangel Michael
who told them that Adam must die, and that there was
no remedy. However, he gave Seth three branches—of
pine, cedar and cypress—which he took to Adam. Adam
wove from these a crown and placed it on his head.'

It will be seen that the Slavonic version differs
in many respects from that of Chumnos. In the
latter Seth alone revisits Paradise, and brings back
from thence three *seeds* which he places in the
mouth of Adam; from these seeds sprout three
trees of pine, cedar and cypress, bound together
in a single stem—clearly symbolic of the Trinity
in Unity. The same idea appears also in Slavonic
apocryphal literature, viz. in the 'Sermo de ligno
crucis,' where Seth brings back a tree from which
sprout three branches of pine, cedar and cypress.
Tischendorf in his Introduction to the *Apocalypsis
Mosis*, p. xi, notes that the legend of Seth sent to
the gates of Paradise to fetch the Oil of Mercy
probably goes back to an early period in the
Christian era, and that it is alluded to by the
author of the *Descensus Christi ad inferos.* The
legend had a considerable vogue in the literature
of the Middle Ages (Tischendorf, p. xi. n. 2)[1].

It may be added that Chumnos's poem occasion-
ally contains echoes from the *Palaea Interpretata*,
e.g. in a passage where Adam is moulded out of

[1] Dr James points out to me that the vision of the weeping
Babe occurs in *Cursor Mundi*, ll. 1340 ff. and also the Babe in
the tree of Paradise is mentioned in R. Morris, *Legends of the
Holy Rood*, pp. 18, 62 ff. (Cf. also Morris's Introduction).

clay taken from 'the four parts.' In the *Palaea* the question is put: 'From what earth was Adam made?' The answer is: 'From Grigot and Gibibn and Cracyn and Tesant.' Jagič, p. 60, cannot explain these terms, and leaves it an open question whether four kinds of earth or four quarters of the earth are meant. Chumnos is equally ambiguous.

This brief discussion of the legends, which I am well aware might be extended almost indefinitely, will, I hope, serve to throw some light upon the features of Chumnos's poem which might at first sight appear strange to Western readers. They are the outcome of a tendency which had long been prevalent in the Nearer East to read into Old Testament story foreshadowings of the New Testament. Some of these tendencies are of course plain in the New Testament itself, and some of the legends, such as that connected with Seth, probably go back to very early in the Christian era, but they were greatly elaborated in the Greek-speaking world as time went on. In the *Palaea Historica* Chumnos's fellow-countryman Andreas, Archbishop of Crete, who died about 730, is frequently cited as an authority, so that the tendency to read New Testament doctrines into the Old Testament must have been prevalent in Crete at least as early as the eighth century. Chumnos's poem is clearly an attempt to make familiar to the masses the subtle interpretations of the *Palaea Interpretata* which had previously been presented in a more popular prose form in the *Palaea Historica*. It is interesting to note how firm a hold these

Greek interpretations took on the Slavonic mind. Passing from Greece through Bulgaria and Serbia they were further elaborated on the soil of Russia, where their popularity is attested by the number of mss surviving from the fifteenth to the eighteenth century. It may also be remarked that in the severer form of the *Palaea Interpretata* this method of O.T. interpretation was a living force in Russia in the fifteenth century. The two principal texts of that work are dated 1406 and 1477 respectively.

Thus Chumnos's poem is no isolated production. It is simply an attempt to popularise the results of theological learning. It is hoped that the reader may be able to judge from the following extracts how far he attained success in his purpose. My own feeling is that he has displayed considerable skill in his selections from the dramatic stories in which the books of Genesis and Exodus abound and that the illustrations are not unworthy of the text.

OLD TESTAMENT LEGENDS

I. ADAM AND EVE EXPELLED FROM PARADISE.
THEY SIGN A BOND FOR THE DEVIL AND TAKE
REFUGE IN THE CAVE OF NEVRON (Fig. 1).

'Therefore ye twain must now depart—punishment
    of your sin,
    No longer may ye do your work this Paradise
      within.'
Then the Archangel order strict upon them both
    did lay,
    That all unclad and all unshod they must from
      thence away.
An angel from the Cherubim stood at the gates
    on guard: 5
    Behind Eve and the first of men the gates were
      shut and barred.
Such was the sentence laid on them, a sentence
    duly kept:
    Before the door of Paradise they sat them down
      and wept.
As Adam sat, in misery he drew full many a groan
    Deep from his inmost heart, and thus he did his
      fate bemoan: 10
'O Paradise, O Paradise, planted for mine own sake,
    From thee, because of my wife's sin, I must
      departure take.'
They rise, and then pursue their way all naked as
    they are,
    And as they walked the savage ground their
      unshod feet did mar.
Darkness they never yet had seen, day had been
    over all,   15
    Now the sun sinks behind the west, and shades
      of evening fall.

I

Τόρα λοιπὸν παγένεται νὰ κάμετε δουλιά σας,
  φύγεται κτὴν παράδεισον, ὡς θέλη ἀνομιά σας.
Ἀρχάγγελος τοὺς ἐπέταξεν ὀγιὰ νὰ καταντήσουν
  ὁλόγυμνους ξυπόλυτους ἔξω τῆς παραδείσου.
Ἄγγελος τάγμα Χερουβὶμ στὲς πόρτες ἐμπο-
  δίζῃ,   5
  τὴν Εὔαν καὶ πρωτόπλαστον ἀπόξω τοὺς σφα-
  λίζῃ.
Ἐπῆραν τὴν ἀπόφασιν Ἀδάμος μὲ τὴν Εὔαν,
  καὶ ἐναντίον τῆς παράδεισος ἐκάτζασιν καὶ
  κλέγαν.
Καθίζῃ Ἀδὰμ ὁ θλιβερὸς καὶ βαραναστενάζῃ,
  καὶ ἀπὸ ψυχῆς ὁδύρετο, δρυμιὰν φωνὴν φωνάζῃ.   10
Παράδεισε ἁγιώτατε, διὰ μέναν φυτεμένος,
  καὶ διὰ τῆς Εὔας τὴν βουλὴν ἀπόξω σφαλισ-
  μένος.
Σικόνουνται, μισεύγουσιν, παγένουν τὴν ὁδόν τους,
  ξηπόλυτοι καὶ ὁλόγυμνοι περιπατοῦν στὸ γόν
  τος.
Σκότος δὲν εἴδασιν ποτέ, εἴχασιν πάντα μέρα,   15
  ὁ ἥλιος ἐβασίλευσεν, πλακόνη τους ἑσπέρα.

And as the shadows fell around, their way they
    could not see,
    The sense of sight was lost to them, they sank
    upon their knee.
They thought that never more for them the day-
    light would arise,
    That evermore with shadows dark evening
    would veil the skies.   20
Sudden the Devil thrice-accursed approached them
    with his wile,
    And full of envy in his heart he sought them
    to beguile.
'Say will ye me a promise make that I may comfort
    give,
    That in the light of sun and moon ye once
    again may live?'
So they, for faint of heart they were, for him a
    bond did sign,   25
    And thus the freedom of themselves and all
    they had resign.
'Ourselves and all that from us come, with thee
    we will hold sway,
    And all that thou commandest us we'll faithfully
    obey.'
But that night passed, and lo! there came the light
    of a new day,
    Another night came on, and lo! that night too
    passed away.   30
So once again in mockery the hopes of the twain
    fled:
    They smote their hands upon their breast and
    bitter tears they shed.

Καὶ φθάνουν τους τὰ σκοτεινά, χάνεται ἡ ὁδός
    τους·
κοντεύγοντας τὰ γόνατα θαμπόνεται τὸ φῶς
    τους,
Πιστεύοντας ποτὲ σαυτοὺς νὰ μὴ ἀνατέλει ἡμέρα,
    μὰ νάνε πάντα σκοτεινά, καὶ νὰ κρατεῖ ἐσπέρα.
Κ᾽ εἰς μιὸν ὁ τρισκατάρατος, ἄκου τὸ τί τοὺς
    κάμνη,   21
    ὁ διάβολος ὁ φθονερὸς εἰς πλάνον πῶς τοὺς βάνη.
Λέγει τους τί μου τάσσεται, καὶ γὼ νὰ σᾶς
    ξιδράμω,
    ἥλιον, φεγγάριν καὶ φῶς ὡραιότατον καὶ μέραν
    νὰ σᾶς κάμω;
Καὶ αὐτοὶ ὀλιγοψυχήσασιν, χειρόγραφον τοῦ κάμ-
    νουν   25
    (εἴ)τια λογὴν τοῦ τάξασιν, λέγουν καὶ ἀναθι-
    βάνουν.
Ἡμεῖς καὶ ὅλα τὰ τέκνα μας μὲ σέναν νὰ κρατοῦμεν,
    κεῖς ὅτι θέλεις μας εἰπεῖν οὐδὲ ποσὸς ναυ-
    γοῦμεν.
Κ᾽ ἡ νύκτα ἐκείνη ἐπέρασεν, κῆλθεν ἄλλη ἡμέρα,
    καὶ πάλιν ἐκείνη ἐπέρασεν, κῆλθεν ἡ ἄλλη
    μέρα.   30
Καὶ ᾽Αδὰμ πάλιν γελάστικεν δεύτερον μὲ τὴν
    Εὔαν,
    τὸ στῆθος τους ἐδέρνασιν, φαρμακεμένα κλέγαν.

And as they walked on night and day, at length
    their footsteps came
  Unto a cavern marvellous, and Nevron was its
    name.
So there they crept in hand in hand, and there
    they made their nest,   35
  Till Death himself should find them out, which
    was their long last rest.

II. CAIN'S ACT OF MURDER DETECTED. THE CURSE LAID UPON HIM. THE BURIAL OF ABEL.

Then on a sudden was the voice of God borne on
    the wind:
  'Where is thy brother, tell Me, Cain, for him
    I fain would find?'
Cain answer made: 'I do not know, his shepherd
    who made me?
  The earth is wide for him to walk, his path
    therein is free.'
'O Cain,' the Voice replied, 'what deed is this
    that thou hast done?   5
  The cry from that blood which thou shed'st
    its way to Me hath won.
Didst thou believe the absorbing earth could hide
    that blood from Me?
  Didst thou believe I knew it not when I asked
    "Where is he?"
A heavy curse is on thee laid that trembling thou
    must fly,
  And from before the face of men to mountains
    waste must hie.'   10

Καὶ μέραν νύκταν περπατοῦν, κεύγάνη τους ὁ
   δρόμος
σὲ σπήλαιον παράξενον, ὄναμαν τοῦ Νευρόνος.
Ἀλλήλως μέσα ἐμπαίνουσιν, κάμνουν τὴν κατοι-
   κιάν τους,   35
ὥστε νὰ τοὺς εὔρη ὁ θάνατος, ὁποῦνε ἡ παροικιά
   τους.

II

Ἦλθεν φωνὴ καὶ συντυχιὰ ἀπὸ θεοῦ στὸν Κάϊν,
   ἐρωτά τον διὰ τὸν ἀδελφόν, τὸ ποῦνε ἢ ποῦ
   πάγη.
Καὶ αὐτὸς ἐπιλογήθηκεν, καὶ νάμ' ἐγὼ βοσκός του;
   ἡ γῆς ἔνε τοῦ μόδου του, καὶ ὁ δρόμος ἐδικός
   του.
Κάϊν, καὶ τί τον τόπικες, σ' αὐτὸν τὸν ἀδελφόν
   σου;   5
τὸ αἷμαν του βοᾷ εἰς ἐμέ, κ' ἡ ἁμαρτία ὀμπρός
   σου.
Ἐθάρης, Κάϊν, δενήξευρα, ὄντεν ἐγὼ εἶπα ποῦσου;
κ' ἡ γῆς αὐτῆ κατάπινε τὸ αἷμαν τ' ἀδελφοῦ
   σου;
Ἐπικατάρατος λοιπὸν νὰ τρέμης καὶ νὰ φεύγης,
   καὶ ἀπὸ τὸ πρόσωπον τῆς γῆς ὄρη βουνὰ νὰ
   ὁδεύης.   10

'But if an exile from this land I'm driven at Thy
  behest,
  I know no spot in all the world where I may
  safely rest,
For whosoe'er shall find me out will me of surety
  slay,
  And no long time together knit will soul and
  body stay.'
'Nay,' said the Lord, 'a promise fixed do I now
  make to thee,   15
  The man that smiteth thee to death shall never
  pardon see.
The burden of thy seven sins he shall upon him
  take,
  The load of all thy wretchedness he shall his
  own load make.'
All quivering like an aspen-leaf he turned himself
  to flight,
  Like hound's in madness changéd were his colour
  and his might.   20
When Adam came and Eve and saw Abel in death
  outlaid,
  They smote their hands upon their breasts and
  lamentation made.
For never yet had either seen a man bereft of
  life,
  Not even at Nature's gentle call, still less in
  violent strife.
The more time passed, so much the more the
  corpse fell to decay.   25
  The frame of Abel who loved God began to rot
  away.

Ἀνὲν καὶ σὺ ζηγόνις με ἀπὸ τὴν γῆν ἀπόσω,
οὐδὲν ἠξεύρω τὸ λοιπὸν νὰ πάγω ἢ ποῦ δόσω.
Καὶ ὁποῖος ἐμὲ νὰ θελ᾽ εὕρην εἰς μιὸν διὰ νὰ
με σφάξῃ,
καὶ τὴν ψυχὴν ἐκ τοῦ κορμιοῦ σύντομα νὰ
πετάξῃ.
Ὄχι, του λέγει ὁ Κύριος σεσὲν νὰ μένε τάξῃ,   15
μὰ νάνε ἀσυγχώρητος ὁποῦ σε θὲ πατάξῃ.
Τὰ ἑπτά σου ἁμαρτήματα καὶ τὲς ταλαιπορίες
νὰ παραλάβῃς στὴν ψυχήν, καὶ ὅλες ταῖς ἁμαρτίαις.
Κ᾽ ἦσε φυγὴν ἐτράπηκεν, καὶ τρέμει σὰν τὸ
φύλλον,
μαύρος πολλὰ καὶ ἀδύναμος σὰν τὸν λυσάριν
σκύλον.   20
Καὶ ἦλθεν κῆβρεν ὁ Ἀδὰμ τὸν Ἄβελ μὲ τὴν Εὔα,
τὸ στῆθος τους ἐδέρνασιν, φαρμακεμένα κλέγα.
Διατὶ ποττὲ δὲν εἴδασιν αὐτοίνοι ἀποθαμένον,
οὐδὲ μὲ θάνατον καλόν, ἀλλ᾽ οὐδε σκοτομένον.
Καὶ ὅσον ἐπέρναν ὁ καιρός, τόσον ἐκαταλιέτον   25
ὁ Ἄβελ ὁ θεοσεβής, ἤρχιζεν καὶ σαπιέτον.

The longer they did gaze on him, more bitterly
    they moaned,
    Faster with hands they beat their breasts, and
      yet more deeply groaned.
Till God in pity did send down an angel to the
    place
    Where Eve in tribulation cried, and Adam hid
      his face.   30
'Why sit ye so,' he said to them, 'why gaze ye
    thus on death,
    Upon an empty shell of man bereft of blood
      and breath?
Nay, take him up and carry him unto the riven
    cave,
    There let this lad all undefiled be laid within
      a grave.
This is that death whereof God spake, when erring
    ye did say   35
    "As gods ourselves have we become and hence-
      forth live for aye.'"
So buried by his parents' hands, Abel in earth
    did lie,
    Many a bitter tear they shed and heaved full
      many a sigh.

III. CAIN SHOT BY THE BLIND LAMECH (Fig. 2).

Methuselah begat Lamech, that brave and stalwart
    lad,
    Blind was he from his earliest years, but great
    the grace he had.

Καὶ ὅσον αὐτὸν ἐυλέπασιν, πλεότερα ἐφονάζα
καὶ ἐκλέγασιν καὶ δέρνουντα καὶ βαραανα-
στενάζα.

Καὶ ἄγγελος ἀπὸ θεοῦ σαυτοὺς ἀποσταλμένος,
ὁποῦ ἡ Εὔα θλίβετον καὶ ὁ Ἀδὰμ ἦτον θλι-
μένος, 30
Τί κάθεσται τοὺς ἔλεγεν, αὐτὸν μὲ δίχος αἷμα
σῶμαν νεκρὸν νὰ υλέπετε, ὁποῦνε δίχος πνεῦμα;
Ἀμέτε τον στὸ σπήλαιον, ὁπόνε τὸ χαράκιν,
καὶ μέσα αὐτόνον θάψεται, τάγιον παλικαράκι.
Αὐτοῦνος ἔνε θάνατος, ὁποῦ Θεὸς σας εἶπε, 35
ὀντὲν ἐσεῖς βαλθήκετε, θεοὶ διὰ να γενῆτε.
Λοιπὸν ἡ μάνα καὶ ὁ πατὴρ τὸν Ἀβελ ἀποθάψαν,
μαναστενάγματα πολλά, κ᾽ οἱ δύο δρυμιὰ τὸν
κλάψαν.

III

Καὶ Μαθουσάλας τὸν Λάμεχ, αὐτὸν τὸ παλλι-
κάρι·
τυφλὸς ἀνεγεννήθηκεν, ἦχεν μεγάλην χάριν.

Four-footed beasts and creeping things, his arrow
    laid them low,
  Wherever bird of heaven did fly, none could
    escape his bow.
A boy he had to guide his hand that he might
    shoot aright,   5
  To put the arrow to the string when he the
    prey would smite.
'Twas he who first of men did take two partners
    of his life ;
  Ada he chose first for himself: Sela was next
    his wife.
He cherished both within his home, to both he
    honour gave,
  And without strife in blissfulness unto the twain
    he clave.   10
Now as it chanced, upon a day he to the field did
    go,
  Together with his youthful guide that he might
    ply the bow.
Unhappy Cain had fled away into a bed of
    reeds,
  And there within their mighty growth he hid
    from his misdeeds.
Now as he shook from very fear the reeds with
    him did shake,   15
  For with the curse which lay on him his heart
    seemed like to break.
The time was drawing on apace, the time for Cain
    to go
  On his last journey to the realms of everlasting
    woe.

Τετράποδα, σιρνάμενα ὅλα νὰ τὰ δοξεύγη,

εἴτις κεῖς τὰ πετούμενα, οὐδένα δέν του φεύγη.

Λοιπὸν ἡ ἐπιστήμη του ἔζεν μὲ τὸ κυνήγη, 5

καὶ οὐδένα ζῶν τοῦ κυνηγιοῦ ἦτον διὰ νὰ τοῦ

φύγη.

Κεῖχεν κοπέλλην ὁδηγὸν τὸ χέρην του νὰ σάζη,

νὰ σύρνη τὴν σαγίτταν του, αὐτοῦνον διὰ νὰ

σφάζη.

Αὐτοῦνος πρῶτος ἔδειξεν γυναῖκες δύο νὰ πέρνουν·

ἐπῆρεν πρῶτα τὴν Ἀδάν, καὶ τὴν Σελὰν τοῦ

φέρνουν. 10

Μ' αὐτούνες ἀνεπ(α)ύετον, εἶχεν τες διὰ δικές

του,

ἐπρόσεχεν καὶ τίμαν τες, διαβλογητικές του.

Μιὰ ἐκ τὲς διαβαζόμενες ἐπῆγεν νὰ θηρεύση,

διαναύρη μὲ τὸν ὁδηγὸν ζῶα να τὰ δοξέψη.

Καὶ ὁ Κάϊς ὁ ταλαίπωρος ἦτον ἀκουμπισμένος 15

σὲ καλαμιόναν θαυμαστὸν εὑρίσκετον χοσμένος.

Καὶ ὁ καλαμιόνας ἐσίετον ἐκ τὴν πολλὴν τρομάραν

τοῦ Κάϊν τοῦ ταλαίπορου ὁποῦχεν τὴν κατάραν.

Said Lamech to his little guide, 'dost mark how
    the reeds shake?
    They shake as when the north wind blows and
        mighty forests quake.   20
Surely some beast is lurking there, my arrow's
    destined prey;
    Come, hasten, from thy quiver draw, lest it
        should slip away.
Direct my aim towards the reeds, steady my hand
    aright,
    That straight into the quarry's lair my bolt may
        wing its flight.'
Back from the bow he drew the string, forth did
    the arrow fly   25
    Into the heart of hapless Cain who uttered one
        sharp cry,
A cry that told of deep despair; his soul sped
    forth in pain.
    Thus found its end the tortured life of miserable
        Cain.
    From the dread cry did Lamech know that he
        a man had slain.
Straightway in bitterness of wrath up to the boy
    he went,   30
    A blow he dealt him from behind, and his life
        too was spent.
'Unwitting have I slain a man,' in anguish thus
    he cries,
    'My fathers' father, and my son—he reft of life
        too lies.
Upon myself Cain's seven sins have I now taken o'er,
    Not these alone; upon me crowd seventy and
        seven more.   35

Ἔσωσεν τότες ὁ καιρὸς ὁ Κάϊς νὰ μισέψη,
κ' ἧς τὴν αἰώνιον κόλασιν νὰ πὰ διὰ ναπλι-
κέψη.   20
Λέγει του Λάμεχ, κάτεχε· βλέπω στὸν καλαμιόνα·
γύνεται τάραξις πολλή, σὰν ὁ βορρὰς λυμιόνα.
Νομίζω νάνε ἐκεῖ θεριὸν ἢ ζῶα διὰ κυνήγην,
καὶ σίρε τὴν σαγίτταν σου, διὰ νὰ μή μας
φύγη.
Λέγει του, σάσε τὴν χεῖραν μου, στῆσε μου τὴν
παλάμην   25
ὁποῦνε τὸ τετράποδον ἀνάντια στὸ καλάμην.
Καὶ σίρνη τὴν σαγίτταν του, κεῖς τὴν καρδιὰν τὸν
σφάζη,
τὸν Κάϊν τὸν ταλαίπορον· δρυμιὰν φωνὴν
φωνάζη.
Ἥτια λογῆς ἐφόναξεν, κ' εὔγικεν ἡ ψυχή του,
καὶ μετ' αὐτὴν ἐπέρασεν ἡ ἔρημος ζωή του.   30
Καὶ ἀπὸ τὸ κρούσμαν ἐγρίκησεν, καὶ σκότοσεν
τὸν Κάϊν,
στὸν ὁδηγόν του σήμοσεν, καὶ μὲ θυμόν του
πάϊν,
Καὶ σφοντιλιάν του κτίπησεν καὶ τὴν ψυχήν του
εὐγάνη.
Ἄνδρα στανιὸν ἐσκότοσα, καὶ τότες τὸν υἱόν μου,
ὁ κύρις ἦτον, κάτεχε, αὐτὸς τῶν γονιῶν μου.   35

Upon me will the wrath of God, my Saviour,
    henceforth rest,
  Ne'er will He welcome me among the number
    of the blest.'
Yet God in mercy him first gave redemption in
    need's hour:
  Pardon He granted and bestowed salvation's
    healing power.

IV. PROMISE OF THE OIL OF MERCY. SETH'S
    JOURNEY TO PARADISE IN QUEST THEREOF.
    DEATH OF ADAM (Figs. 3—6).

Third on the first-created man the Lord did turn
    His wrath,
  And upon him as upon Eve a bitter curse sent
    forth.
'With fiery trial of toil and pain thy days shall
    ever burn,
  To Eden and its Paradise never shalt thou return.
Thorny shall be thy road, thy path shall thistles
    sharp beget,   5
  Anguish and never-ceasing moan shall all thy
    life beset.
As with dust taken from the ground I first did
    fashion thee,
  So to that dust shalt thou return, there shall thy
    dwelling be.
But oil of purest purple stain, the oil of Mercy
    kind,
  One of Ourselves in future time, in humbleness
    of mind,   10

Ὄχι μόνον παράλαβα τὲς ἑπτά του ἀνομίες,
μὰ εὐδομηκονταεὐτὰ ἔλαβα ἁμαρτίαις.
Καὶ θέλω πειραχθὴν πολλὰ εἰς τὸν Θεὸν σωτῆρα,
καὶ οὐ ποσὸς με θε δεκτήν, μαυτοῦνον νάχω
μοῖραν.
Λοιπὸν αὐτοῦνος ἔδειξεν πρώτην ἐξαγωρίαν,   40
καὶ ἀπὸ Θεοῦ συγχώρησιν· ἔλαβεν σωτηρίαν.

IV

Τρίτον κ᾽ εἰς τὸν πρωτόπλαστον ἀρχίζη ναπονάται,
καὶ μὲ μεγάλον του θυμὸν σεκεῖνον καταράται.
Μὲ λύπες καὶ ἀναστεναγμοὺς πολλὰ νὰ παραδύρης,
κεῖς τὸν Ἐδὲμ παράδεισον πλέον νὰ μὴ
διαγύρης.
Ἀκάνθες νάνε στράτα σου, τριυόλια ἡ ὁδός
σου,   5
κριτήρια καὶ ἀναστεναγμοὺς ὀπίσω σου καὶ
ὀμπρός σου.
Μὲ γῆν καὶ χόμαν ἔπλασα αὐτὴν τὴν ἑλικιάν σου,
σαυτίνην πάλιν νὰ στραφῆς, καὶ νάνε κατοικιά
σου.
Λάδιν τὸ πορφυρότατον, τὸ λέγουν λεημοσύνην,
εἰς τὸν ἐρχόμενον καιρὸν με ταπεινοφροσύ-
νην,   10

M   2

Shall at My bidding bear to thee, that therewithal
    death's sting
  He may remove and of thy sin forgetfulness
    may bring.
In form of pine and cedar-wood and of the cypress
    tree,
  Spreading towards the East and West I shall be
    raised for thee.
It is the will of God that thou one of Ourselves
    shalt be,   15
  Albeit that from Paradise thou must all-naked
    flee.'
    *   *   *   *   *   *   *

So he begat a son named Seth, he was a child of
    blessing,
  Ever God's justice, majesty and perfect grace
    confessing.
Adam and Eve he honoured well, obedient to
    their call,
  And so God blessed him: he was great before
    the eyes of all.   20
Now God was minded soon to take Adam unto
    his rest.
  He sent him pains that racked his head, and he
    was sore distrest.
He called his son Seth to his side (listen to what
    he bad),
  His eyes did overflow with tears as he embraced
    the lad.
'Depart, my son, to Paradise, that there thou
    mayest greet   25
  The angel called the Cherubin, and fall low at
    his feet.

Εἷς ἀπομᾶς θέλει φανή, καὶ αὐτούνων θέλω πέψην,
νὰ λάβῃ θάνατον ἀπὸ σὲ διὰ νὰ σε ξεμνη-
στέψῃ.
Εἰς πεύκον, κέδρον, κάτεχε, σαυτὸν τὸ κυπαρίσσιν,
γιασέναν θέλω ὑψωθῇ σ' ἀνατολὴν καὶ δύσιν.
Εἷς ἀπομᾶς ἐθέλησε Θεὸς διὰ νὰ γένη,   15
καὶ ἀπέξω τῆς παράδεισος ὁλόγυμνος εὐγέν(η).

*   *   *   *   *   *   *

Ἐγέννησεν λοιπὸν τὸν Σήθ, ἄνδραν εὐλογημένον,
τὸν δίκαιον καὶ θεοσεβῆ καὶ τὸν χαριτωμένον.
Ἦτον πολλὰ τῆς ἐπακοῆς Ἀδάμ τε καὶ τῆς Εὔας,
κ' εὐλόγησέν τον ὁ Θεός, κῆτον εἰς ὅλους
μέγας.   20
Καὶ ὁ Κύριος ἐνθυμήθηκεν νὰ πάρι τὸν Ἀδάμι,
δίδη του κεφαλόπονον, δὲν ξέρη τί νὰ κάμη.
Τὸν Σὴθ ἐπαρακάλεσεν, καὶ ἄκου τί ἀναθηβάνη,
τὰ μάτια του ἐνορκόσασιν, καὶ αὐτὸν περιλαμπάνη.
Σήρε, του λέγει, εἰς παράδεισον, λόγον διὰ νὰ
μηλήσης   25
στὸν ἄγγελον τὸν Χερουνίμ, καὶ νὰ τὸν προσ-
κυνήσης.

Address him for my sake and pray that he to thee
    may give
    That oil whereof God spake to me, the oil by
    which men live.'
'O father Adam, let it be as thou commandest
    me,
    I shrink not from the road, although toilsome
    and rough it be.   30
One thing I lack—I do not know the paths that
    thither lead.
    Show me the way, and forthwith there I hie
    with all my speed.'
'Take thou the broad and rising road, follow it to
    the end,
    And ever bear towards the right, for so the
    track doth bend.
Towards the rising of the sun, thither thy road
    pursue,   35
    Till Eden and its Paradise do burst upon thy
    view.
And as thou goest on thy way, footprints will
    surely show,
    Mine and thy mother's, not a blade of grass on
    these can grow,
All for the sake of that dread sin the which I did
    commit,
    When in my disobedience I God's ordinance
    did quit.'   40
Then Seth to traverse did begin the road where
    he was sent,
    And to the east he set his face, and towards the
    right hand went.

Καὶ νὰ τοῦ πῆς διαλλόγου μου, γιὰ νὰ παρα-
καλέσῃς
τὸ λάδιν ὁ Θεὸς τὸ μούδιξεν, ὀγιὰ νὰ με φελέσῃ.
Πάτερ Ἀδάμ, μετὰ χαρὰς στὸν ὁρισμόν σου νάνε,
καὶ δὲν βαριοῦμε τὴν ὁδόν, καλὰ μακρὰ καὶ
νάνε.   30
Μὰ τοῦτον δισκολεύγομαι, γιὰ νὰ μὴ δὲν κατέχω,
μὰ βάλε με εἰς ὁδηγιάν, καὶ γὼ γοργὸν νὰ
τρέχω.
Ἔπαρε τ᾽ ἀναβάσταμαν, τὴν στράταν τὴν μεγάλην,
καὶ κράτε πάντα σου δεξιά, ὅπου ἡ ὁδὸς σὲ
εὐγάλη,
Ὅπου ἀνατέλλη ἥλιος, ἐκεῖ κάμε νὰ ὁδεύῃς,   35
καὶ τῆς Ἐδὲμ ὁ παράδεισος, τοὺς δρόμους διὰ
ναυγένῃς.
Καὶ θέλῃς εἰδεῖν πατιματιὲς ἐμὲν καὶ τῆς μητρός
σου,
χόρτον δένενε μπορετὸν αὐτοῦ να ξεφυτρόσῃ,
Μόνον διὰ τὴν παράβασιν αὐτίνην τὴν ἐπίκα,
ἐκ τοῦ Θεοῦ τὸν ὁρισμὸν καὶ ὑπακοῆς εὐγίκα. 40
Ἄρχησεν τότε ὁ Σὴθ τὴν στράταν διὰ ναυγένη,
στὰ μέρη τῆς ἀνατολῆς δεξιὰ διὰ νὰ παγένη.

So day and night he journeyed on, and Eden's
    bounds he sought ;
    After long toil his footsteps nigh to Paradise
      were brought.
He saw the Archangel standing there as guardian
    of the door,   45
    And in his hand with blade full keen a whetted
      sword he bore.
At sight of his majestic mien Seth was o'ercome
    with dread,
    His tongue did stammer and his heart fainted
      and seemed as dead.
With mighty trembling of the limbs before him
    low he knelt,
    And down he bowed his head until his forehead
      the ground felt.   50
Fear laid its hold so fast on him that o'er his
    cheeks tears ran.
    At length with awe and reverence his message
      he began.
'Hail to thee, Archangel of God, thou warden of
    his host,
    Who brighter than the sun the rule of Paradise
      dost boast.
Hail to thee, Cherubin divine, like blazing fire
    thou art :   55
    Thy sword e'en now with piercing stroke hath
      darted through my heart.
Adam my sire and mother Eve this message send
    to thee—
    To thee whose fearful aspect all worship on
      bended knee—

Μέραν καὶ νύκταν περπατῇ πρὸς τῆς Ἐδὲμ τὸν
τόπον,
καὶ σώνη στὸν παράδεισον μετὰ μεγάλον κόπον.
Καὶ ὑλέπει τὸν ἀρχάγγελον στὴν πόρταν κουμπι-
σμένον, 45
βαστάνη κ᾽ εἰς τὸ χέριν του σπαθὴν ἀκονη-
μένον.
Τὸ νὰ τὸν δὴ τὸ ὑλέμαν του, ὁ Σὴθ τὸν ἐδηλιάσεν,
μέσα ψυχή του κρύφθηκεν, τὰ λόγια του ἐχάσεν.
Καὶ μὲ μεγάλον τρόμασμα ὀμπρός του γονατίζη,
καὶ τὸ κεφάλην του κλίνεν, χαμὲ στὴν γῆν
τογγίζη. 5c
Καὶ ἀπὸ τὸν φόβον τὸν πολὺν ἤρχισε διὰ νὰ
κλέγη,
καὶ μὲ πολλὴν εὐλάβειαν ἀρχίζη νὰ τοῦ λέγει.
Χαῖρε Θεοῦ ἀρχάγγελε καὶ μέγα ταξιάρχη,
καὶ λάμπῃς πλεότερα ἡλίου, τοῦ παραδείσου
κρατάρχη.
Χαῖρε ὁ θεῖος Χερουβίμ καὶ φλόγα, ἡ ῥομφαία 55
ὁποῦ σταδά μου τὴν καρδιάν ἐμπίκεν σὰν
καρφέα.
Ἀδάμος ὁ πατέρας μου κ᾽ ἡ Εὖα σοῦ μηνοῦσι,
τὸ φουερόν σου ἀνάυλεμα ὅλοι τὸ προσκυνοῦσι,

O wilt thou pray the Lord for them that he in
    mercy give
    That oil of purest purple stain, to anoint them-
    selves therewith?'   60
The Archangel said 'Seth, turn aside and look
    within the gate,
    But see thou enter not therein and challenge
    divine fate.
Thou wilt behold all kinds of fruit and wondrous
    colours blent,
    And flowers rare beyond compare, apples of
    sweetest scent:
Many another marvel too, many a famous
    sight,   65
    Waters which flow unceasingly and streams of
    milky white.'
So Seth did turn aside and all that rose above
    surveyed,
    And that great vision marvellous deep to his
    heart he laid.
He saw an awesome stream therein, parted in
    rivers four,
    Each river held its separate way with a deep-
    sounding roar.   70
Hard by the river-banks there rose a tree ex-
    ceeding tall,
    Wherewith the serpent had deceived his mother
    to her fall.
Wild beasts of every tribe and kind were gathered
    all around,
    About the roots of that high tree they couched
    upon the ground.

Νὰ δεηθῆς τὸν Κύριον σαυτοὺς νὰ ξαποστείλη
λάδιν τὸ πορφυρότατον νὰ τὸ λουστοῦν ὡς
φίλοι. 60
Λέγει του, Σήθ, παράσκιψε καὶ 'δὲ ἀπὸ τὴν θύραν,
καὶ ὑλέπεσε νὰ μὴν ἐμπῆς διὰ τοῦ Θεοῦ τὴν
μοίραν.
Καὶ θὲς ἰδεῖν καρποὺς πολλοὺς καὶ δένδροι πλου-
μισμέν(α)
καὶ ἄλλους ἀνθοὺς παράξενους καὶ μύλα μυρι-
σμένα,
Καὶ ἄλλα πολλὰ θαυμάσματα ἐξακουστὰ μεγάλα,
καὶ τὰ νερὰ τρεχάμενα, ἄσπρα ὁσὰν τὸ γάλα. 66
Καὶ ὁ Σήθης ἐπαράσκηψεν, καὶ ὅλα τὰ πάνω
βλέπη,
καὶ ὅλα καλὰ τὰ σκόπησεν, καὶ ὁ νούς του
ταναδέκτη.
Βλέπη ποτάμιν φουερόν, κ' εἰς τέσσερα μοιράζη,
πᾶσα ποτάμιν ξέχορα τὸν δρόμον του ἀνα-
κράζη. 70
Κεῖδεν δένδρον πολλὰ ψιλὸν σιμὰ πρὸς τὸ ποτάμιν,
ὁποῦ τὴν Εὔαν ἐδόλεψεν ὁ ὄφις στὸ καλάμιν.
Κῆσαν θεριὰ πᾶσα λογῆς ἄγρια καὶ τριγυρίζα
αὐτούνον τὸ ψιλὸν δενδρόν, ἀποκοντὰ στὴν
ῥίζαν. 74

The bark had fallen to the earth o'erspun with
    spider's weft;   75
  The tree was dry and desolate and of all leaves
    was reft.
Seth looked upon the sight so strange, listen to
    what befell,
  He turned and asked the angel-guard, who
    thus his tale did tell.
The Angel said, 'Seth, turn again, and once more
    raise thine eye,
  And when thou markest what is there, again to
    me reply.'   80
Then Seth once more his head did turn, again the
    tree marked well,
  Demons were swarming everywhere whose
    numbers none could tell.
There in the midst of Paradise he looked at the
    tree's roots,
  Down to the bottom of the abyss its fibres deep
    it shoots.
And lo! on the tree-top a babe, and swaddling
    bands he wears.   85
  That babe incessantly did weep unmeasurable
    tears.
Again Seth to the Angel turned, again he told
    him all,
  How from the eyes of that sweet babe tears
    without end did fall.
'As for that babe thou see'st aloft, that weepeth
    over there,
  Amid the high boughs of the tree, that tree
    accursed and bare,   90

Ἀραχνιασμένον ἦτονε τὸ φλούδιν τουππεσμένον,
ἦτον ξερὸν παντέρημον, τὰ φύλλα μαδισμένον.
Βλέποντας τὸ παράξενον, ἄκου τὸ τίν τα κάμνη·
διαγέρνη πρὸς τὸν ἄγγελον, καὶ ὅλα ταναθιβάνη.
Λέγει του, Σήθ, ὁ ἄγγελος, διάγυρε πάλιν, δέ το,
καὶ ὅτι καὶ ἀδὴς πάλιν σ᾽ αὐτόν, ἔλα, σε μέναν
εἰπέ το.   80
Καὶ πάλιν ξαναδιάγυρεν, στοχάζεται τὸ δένδρον,
βλέπη δαιμόνια ρίφνητα, ὁποῦ δένηχα μέτρον.
Βλέπει τὲς ρίζες τοῦ δενδροῦ, μέσα τῆς παραδείσου,
καὶ αὐτοῦνες κάτω ξεπερνοῦν στὰ βάθη τῆς
ἀβύσσου.
Καὶ ἔναν παιδάκιν φασκιοτὸν εἰς τὴν κορφὴν τοῦ
δένδρου,   85
ὡς νήπιον βιζανόμενον ἔκλεγεν δίχος μέτρον.
Δεύτερον πάλιν διάγυρεν στὸν ἄγγελον καὶ λέγει
διὰ ὅλα τὰ γινόμενα, καὶ τὸ παιδὶν πῶς κλέγει.
Λέγει του, αὐτοῦνον τὸ παιδὶν ὁποῦ θωρῆς καὶ
κλέγει,
καὶ κείτεται πρὸς τὴν κορφὴν στὸ δένδρον
ὁποῦ φλέγει,   90

That is the Son of God who weeps that Adam did
    offend,
    And for the sin of Eve would fain down to the
    earth descend.
One day He shall to earth come down and there
    salvation give:
    His name is Mercy, He will grant new laws
    that men may live.'
He handed him three seeds, and then these words
    he bade him hear: 95
    'Thy father Adam, know it well, to death is
    drawing near.
Within three days of thy return the first-created
    man,
    I tell thee of a truth, will pass beneath death's
    awful ban.
Bury thy father where he is, within that cavern
    riven,
    And lay within his mouth those seeds that I to
    thee have given.   100
A trilogy of branches will from these three seeds
    arise,
    One stem, with triple root, shall lift three
    boughs unto the skies.
One bough shall be of pine-tree wood, cypress the
    next shall be,
    The third the sweetness shall exhale of noble
    cedar-tree.'
Forth from the bounds of Paradise Seth started
    on his way,   105
    Seeking the eastern parts wherein the place of
    Nevron lay.

Αὐτόνε Θεοῦ υἱός, κλέγει διὰ τὸν Ἀδάμι,
  καὶ διὰ τῆς Εὔας τὸ κακόν, βούλεται διὰ νὰ
    δράμη,
Καὶ ὀντ᾽ἂν αὐτὸς νὰ κατεβῇ, τὸν κόσμον διὰ νὰ
    σώσῃ.
  αὐτὸς ἔνε τὸ ἔλεος, νέον νόμον νὰ δόσῃ.
Τρία σπιράκια τούδοκεν, καὶ ἄκου τί ἀναθη-
    βάνη.   95
  κάτεχε, τὸν πατέρα σου, θνήσκει, παραλαμ-
    βάνης,
Ἡσὲ τρεῖς ἡμέρες, λέγω σου, ὅταν ἐσὺ νὰ σώσῃς,
  ἤξευρε τοῦ πρωτόπλαστου θάνατος θέλη δόσῃ.
Καὶ θάψαι τὸν πατέρα σου στὸ σπήλαιον στὰ
    χαράκια,
  καὶ βάλε του εἰς τὸ στόμαν του τούτα τὰ τρία
    σπιράκια.   100
Τρία κλονάρια τρίλογα θέλουσι ξεφυτρώσῃ,
  ἔναν κορμὴν με τρὶς κορφές, τρὶς ῥίζες (δ)ὲν
    κεντρώσῃ.
Ἡ μιὰ κορφὴ τοῦ πεύκουνε, κ᾽ ἡ ἄλλη κυπαρίσσῃ,
  ἡ τρίτος κέδρος φουμιστός, μ᾽ αὐτοῦνα νὰ
    μυρίσῃ.
Ἐξεύην ἐκ τὸν παράδεισον, κεὐγάνη τον ὁ δρό-
    μος   105
  στὰ μέρη τῆς ἀνατολῆς, στὸν τόπον τοῦ Νευ-
    ρῶνος.

And there he saw his parents dear who with an
　　anxious heart
　　Waited the coming of that son that did from
　　home depart.
And when Seth saw their face again, he let drop
　　joyous tears,
　　For that he brings a message home, salvation's
　　news he bears.　　　　　　　　　　　　　110
'O parents mine, all bliss and joy attend you on
　　this day,
　　My honoured sire and mother dear for whom
　　I ever pray.'
He spake of all those fateful words which the
　　Archangel told,
　　What he had with his own eyes seen, what
　　future ages hold.
Adam for thrice a hundred years, add to these
　　thirty more,　　　　　　　　　　　　　115
　　Had ever been downcast and sad, never a smile
　　he wore;
But when in humbleness of heart he heard salva-
　　tion's news,
　　Comfort he had, and smiles of joy his careworn
　　face diffuse.
He raised aloft his hands and blessed the great
　　Creator's name,
　　With consolation in his breast he called for
　　Death, who came.　　　　　　　　　　　120
For as the Archangel prophesied that he should
　　shortly die,
　　On the third day from Seth's return Adam in
　　earth did lie.

Ἐκεῖδεν τοὺς γονέους του, καὶ ὁμάδι συνοδεύαν,
διαλόγου του ἐλογιάζασι Ἀδάμος μὲ τὴν Εὔαν.
Καὶ αὐτὸς ἐκ τὴν πολλὴν χαρὰν ἀρχίζη διὰ νὰ
κλέγη,
διατί βαστὰ τὸ μήνυμα τῆς σωτηρίας νὰ
λέγει.   110
Χαρὰ νάνε πολλὴ σε σᾶς ἐτούτην τὴν ἡμέραν,
μητέρα ποθινότατη, καὶ τίμιέ μου πατέρα.
Ὅλα τοὺς τὰ διγήθηκεν τ' ἄκουσεν ταρχαγγέλου,
καὶ τά δεν με τὰ μάτια του, καὶ κεῖνα ποῦ τοῦ
μέλλου.
Τριακόσιους χρόνους κάτεχε ἀκόμη καὶ ἄλλους
τράντα,   115
Ἀδάμος δὲν ἐγέλασεν, μάτον θλιμμένος πάντα.
Καὶ ἀκούοντας ὁ ταπεινὸς καὶ ὀλπίζει σωτηρία,
ἐγέλασεν, κ' ἐχάρικεν, κεῖχεν παρηγορία.
Ἐσήκοσεν τὰ χέρια του, τὸν Ποιητὴν δοξάζει,
καὶ μὲ πολλὴν θαράπαψιν τὸν θάνατόν του
κράζη.   120
Καὶ κατὰ πὸς ὁ ἄγγελος εἶπε διὰ ναποθάνη,
στρίτον ἡμέραν τὸν Ἀδὰμ ἡ γῆς παραλαμβάνη.

Within his mouth he placed the seeds, and quickly
    they took root,
  And ere long time had passed away there grew
    a triple shoot.
A year sped by and they increased in beauty and
    in height,   125
  Fairer than any other trees they forced their
    way to light.
One stem they had in common, but the heads did
    part in three,
  The triple roots, though separate, in vigour did
    agree.
A thousand years, a hundred more (no lie with
    me is found),
  Add two and fifty, still within that mouth they
    kept their ground.   130
And by the grace of God they grew throughout
    that long time's stress,
  Ever unblasted they remained, and never were
    seen less.
And each alike of those three trees his own sweet
    perfume breathed,
  That Trinity in Unity three crowns of beauty
    wreathed.

Μέσα λοιπὸν στὸ στόμαν του ἔβαλεν τὰ σπηράκια,
κ'ἦσε λιγούστζικον κερὸν τρία εὐγένου υλαστα-
ράκια.

Κ' εἰς ἕναν χρόνον αὐξένουσιν ὡραία καὶ μεγάλα,
κεῖχασιν πλεὰν τὴν ὀμορφιὰν παρὰ τὰ δένδρα
τ' ἄλλα.   126

Ἕναν κορμὴν μὲ τρὶς κορφὲς ἦσαν ξεχορισμένες,
κ' ἡ ρίζες εἰς τριὰ μοιράζουντα, κῆσαν χαριτω-
μένες.

Χιλίων λέγω καὶ ἑκατὸν χρόνους μὲ δίχος ψ(ό)μα,
ἀκόμη καὶ πεντίντα δυὸ ἦσαν σ'αὐτὸν τὸ
στόμα.   130

Καὶ ἀπὸ τὴν χάριν τοῦ Θεοῦ αὐξάνου, δὲν λιγένουν,
ἀμένε εἰς μιὰν ποσότητα κεῖς ἕναν πάντα
μένουν.

Καὶ πᾶσα ἕναν στὲς κορφὲς ἔχει τὴν μυροδιάν
του,
τὰ τρίλογα καὶ ἕναν κορμὴν χώρια τὴν ὀμορφιάν
του.

V. ENOCH INSCRIBES THE STORY OF THE CREATION ON MARBLE TABLETS (Fig. 7).

And Seth himself begat offspring and blessing on
    them lay,
    Many a daughter, many a son within his home
      did play.
All these he by example taught that they should
    love the Lord,
    And that all wickedness and sin by them should
      be abhorred.
Two men there were of blessing great that issued
    from that race,   5
    These above others feared the Lord and had
      surpassing grace.
The first was Enoch who of God to heaven trans-
    lated went,
    And when the flood o'erwhelmed the earth to
      Paradise was sent.
Full many years with zeal against the giants he
    did burn,
    That they might put their trust in God and to
      repentance turn.   10
But when he saw their heart was hard and sin on
    sin incurred,
    And that through lustfulness of mind against
      themselves they erred,
He reckoned that a blazing fire would the whole
    earth consume,
    Or that the floods would be unbound and send
      the world to doom.

V

Ἐγέννησεν καὶ αὐτὸς ὁ Σὴθ πολλὴν τεκνολογία,

ἀρσενικὰ καὶ θηλυκὰ κεῖχασιν εὐλογία.

Ὅλους αὐτοὺς ἐδίδαξεν νὰν εἰς θεοσεβεία,

νὰ λύπουσιν ἀκ τὰ κακὰ καὶ ἀπὸ τὴν ἀνομίαν.

Μέσα αὐτοὺς εὐγίκασιν δύο ἄνδρες εὐλογημένη,   5

εἴχασιν θεοσέβειαν πολλὰ χαριτωμένη.

Ἥτονε λέγω ὁ Ἐνὼχ ὁποῖος ἐμετετέθη,

στὴν συμφορὰν κατακλυσμοῦ σπαράδεισον

ἐπεύθη.

Αὐτὸς πάντα κοπίαζεν χρόνους διὰ τοὺς γιγάντες,

διὰ νὰ πιστέψουν εἰς Θεόν, νὰ ἐπιστρέψουν

πάντες.   10

Καὶ ὡς εἶδεν τὴν σκληροκαρδιὰν καὶ πᾶσα ἀνομία,

γιὰ νάνε σάρκαπεθυμιά, σαυτούνους ἁμαρτία,

Ἐλόγιασεν ἀπὸ φωτιὰς ἡ γῆς θέλει χαλάση,

ἢ ἀπὸ συμφορὰν νεροῦ ἄβυσσος νὰ κοχλάση.

So taking marble slabs he wrote the things that
    God did make,   15
  The story of the Creator's works and all the
    words He spake.
The strength of marble he used thus his record
    for to write,
  Since that he knew full well defies Time's all
    devouring might.
E'en should there come a blazing fire, it would
    from that refrain,
  Or if a flood o'erwhelmed the earth, these
    tablets would remain.   20

VI. THE CONVERSION OF ABRAM (Figs. 8–10).

Now Terah graven images to worship was inclined,
  And to that worship Abram too did turn his
    youthful mind.
And from his father he did learn much of as-
    tronomy,
  But by that learning he was schooled in God's
    economy.
Next from the progeny of Ham was Hagar born
    a slave,   5
  Whom in the market to Abram the price of
    silver gave.
From Japheth's house and lineage the mighty
    Nevron came,
  Who founded splendid Babylon, that town of
    world-wide fame.
  A stalwart column of defence did men this
    Nevron name.

Ἐπιάσεν καὶ ὅλα τά γραψεν Θεοῦ τὰ μεγα-
   λεῖα,   15
ὁδιὰ τὴν κοσμογέννησιν καὶ θεῖαν ὁμιλίαν.
Αὐτοῦνος ὁκονόμησεν τοὺς μαρμαρένους λίθους
   διὰ νὰ γράψῃ τ' ἄνοθεν εἰς μάρμαρα κεῖς
   λίθους.
Ἀνένε στίας συμφορά, ἡ πλύνθοι νὰ γλυτόσουν,
   ἢ δένε σύγκλησις νεροῦ, τὰ μάρμαρα νὰ
   σώσου.   20

VI

Αὐτὸς ὁ Θάρας τὸν καιρὸν ἐκεῖνον δωλολάτρη,
   σ' αὐτὴν τὴν γνώμην καὶ Ἀυραὰμ καμπόσον
   ἐποκράτη.
Καὶ ἀπὸ τὸν κήρην του ἔμαθεν πολλὴν ἀστρο-
   νομίαν,
   σαυτὴ καλὰ διδάχθηκεν Θεοῦ οἰκονομίαν.
Καὶ ἀπὸ τοῦ Χὰμ τὰ πόγονα ἡ Ἄγαρ ἐγεννήθη, 5
   ὡς σκλάβαν ἀπὸ τὴν ἀγορὰν τοῦ Ἀυραὰμ
   ἐκλήθη.
Καὶ ἀπὸ τοῦ Ἰάφεθ τὰ παιδιὰ ὁ Νευρὼν ἐγενήθη.
Αὐτόνως ἔνε ἀπόκτισεν μεγάλην Βαβυλῶνα,
   κῆτον εἰς ὅλους δυνατός, ἴσως ὡς ἂν κολόνα.

'Twas he that first with measuring wand parcelled
    out sea and land,   10
  And to gods made by mortal hands assigned
    rule and command.
No people now on earth was found homage to
    God to pay,
  But all at shrines idolatrous their sacrifice did
    lay.
Terah himself these images did make with sculp-
    tor's hand,
  But the true meaning of his work he could not
    understand.   15
His custom was that he should send Abram his
    work to take
  Unto the market, and by sale his living thus to
    make.
As Abram went upon his way he looked at
    heaven's wide span:
  In contemplation of its hosts to praise them he
    began.
He saw the glorious sun and moon, and at the
    stars he gazed: 20
  The thought of their great Ruler's power did
    make him sore amazed.
An eager yearning filled his soul to know Him
    and His way,
  To Him as to the one true God homage com-
    plete to pay.
And the Creator, when He saw the longing of that
    soul,
  Did send an angel to reveal the meaning of the
    whole.   25

Αὐτὸς ἐδιομέτρησεν θάλασσαν καὶ τὸν κόσμον, 10
καὶ ἔδωκεν κεῖς τὰ εἴδωλα πίστιν καὶ μέγαν
νόμον.
Καὶ δὲν εὑρέθηκεν λαὸς Θεὸν διὰ νὰ ὀνομάζουν,
μὰ δώθησαν εἰς τὰ εἴδωλα ὅλοι νὰ θυσιάζουν.
Αὐτὸς ὁ Θάρας ἤτονε μάστορας γλυφτολόγος, 14
ὁπούκαμνεν τὰ εἴδωλα γλυφτὰ μὲ δίχος λόγον.
Εἶχεν συνήθειαν ὁ Ἀυραὰμ αὐτὰ διὰ νὰ φέρνη
στὸν φόρον διὰ νὰ τὰ πουλή, καὶ νρῶσι διὰ νὰ
πέρνη.
Καὶ πηγένοντα τὴν στράταν του ἀρχίζει νὰ
λογιάζη
τὰ ἔργα ὁποῦ στὸν οὐρανόν, μὲ πίστην τὰ
δοξάζη.
Τὸν ἥλιον βάλλει εἰς λογισμόν, τάστροι καὶ τὸ
φεγγάρη,   20
πιὸς νάνε ποῦ τὰ κιβερνά, κέχει τὴν τόσιν
χάριν.
Καὶ ὁ λογισμός του ἐγέμησεν νὰ μάθη διὰ τὸν
κτίστην,
ὡς ἂν Θεὸν ἀληθινόν, σαυτὸν νὰ δώση πίστην.
Καὶ ὡς εἶδεν ὁ δημιουργὸς τὴν τόσιν προθυμία,
ἄγγελον ἔπεψεν σαυτόν, δίδη του ἑρμηνία. 25

'Depart,' said He, 'from out thy place, leave behind
    kith and kin,
  And see thou seekest not again thy former
    home to win.
Remove thyself into the land which I shall show
    to thee,
  And as for those that dwell therein they shall
    before thee flee.
The people that from Ham is born is unto thee
    a foe,   30
  And at thy bidding it shall bow and at thy
    bidding go.
Its destined place I will assign, but thou thrice
    blesséd art,
  To thee and after to thy seed My words I will
    impart.
Thy seed shall grow and multiply as sand beside
    the sea,
  As are the stars for multitude so shall thy
    offspring be.   35
Whoever curseth thee and thine, he shall be
    cursed in sin,
  Whoever blesseth thee and thine, he too shall
    blessing win.'
Unto his father's house again Abram with joy
    did hie,
  He humbly bent his knee and then low at his
    feet did lie.
'O father mine, take knowledge of the God I oft
    desired,   40
  Albeit that to idols vain I formerly aspired.

Μήσεψε ἀπὸ τὸν τόπον σου, καὶ ἀπὸ τοὺς συγ-
γενεῖς σου,
καὶ βλέπεσε μὴ δὲν στραφῆς στὸ σπίτην ὅπου
ἦσου.
Κάμε νὰ πάγης εἰς τὴν γῆν ὁποῦ σοῦ θέλω δείξη,
καὶ ὅσοι σεκείνην κατοικοῦν, θέλω τοὺς ἐξα-
λείψη.
Διατὶ ὁ λαὸς ἀπὸ τοῦ Χάμ, ὁποῦνε σὰς ἐχθρός
σας, 30
ἐσέναν καὶ τῶν τέκνων σου νάνε στὸν ὁρισμόν
σας.
Σαυτοὺς τὸν τόπον νὰ φανῶ, καὶ θέλω σοῦ μιλήση,
ἐσέναν καὶ τὸ σπέρμαν σου, θέλω σας εὐλο-
γήσει.
Καὶ αὐτοίνοι νὰ πληθύνουσιν σὰν ἄμμος τῆς
θαλάσσης,
ὡς τ᾽ ἄστρα ποῦνε πολλά, αὐτοὶ καὶ τὰ καλά
σου. 35
Καὶ ὅπιος ἐσᾶς καταραθή, νάνε καταραμένος,
καὶ ὅπιος σας θέλη εὐχηθήν, νάνε εὐλογημένος.
Ἐμετάστρεψεν ὁ Ἀυραὰμ στὸ σπίτην τοῦ πατρός
του,
καὶ μὲ χαρὰν ἀπλέροτην ἐγονάτησεν ὀμπρός του.
Ἔξευρε σὺ πατέρα μου Θεὸν τὸν ἐπεθύμουν, 40
ἀνκαλὰ καὶ γὼ τὰ εἴδωλα προτήτερα προσκύνου.

He bade me from my home depart and leave my
    native plot,
  And henceforth in its vanities have neither part
    nor lot.
He bade me turn to a new land which He to me
    would show:
  He for my sake from out that land would drive
    out every foe.   45
We must forgather, I and mine, thither our
    journey make,
  That in the distant country we our heritage
    may take.'
Terah thereto did answer make (mark well the
    words he speaks)—
  His eyes were brimming o'er with tears that
    trickled down his cheeks—
'God hast thou found, to Him alone homage and
    worship pay,   50
  To idols that are graved with hand henceforth
    thou must say nay.
Serve not those gods of wood and stone to which
    I bent the knee,
  For I have found that all I served are nought
    but vanity.
Thy brother, well thou knowest this, was all
    consumed in sin,
  Dead is thy mother, as for me my heart is
    seared within.   55
Thou art my sole remaining joy, the brightness
    of mine eyes,
  Old am I, feeble in my years, my path for me
    devise.'

Καὶ εἶπεν μου ἀπὸ τὸν τόπον μας καὶ σπίτην σου
    νὰ πέχω,
καὶ ἀποῦ τὰ πράματα αὐτοῦ ποσὸς νὰ μὴν
    μετέχω.
Καὶ νὰ στραφῶ σαυτὴν τὴν γῆν, ὁποῦ μου θέλη
    δείξη,   44
καὶ ὅσοι θέλουστεν ἐχθροί, θέλω τοὺς ἐξαλείψει.
Ἡσαυτήνη νὰ περμαζοκτώ, ὀγιὰ νὰ καταντήσω,
ἐγὼ καὶ ὅλα τὰ τέκνα μου, νὰ τὴν κλερονομήσω.
Καὶ αὐτὸς τοῦ ἀπολογήθηκεν, ἄκου καὶ τί τοῦ
    λέγει,
τὰ μάτια του γεμόσασιν, καὶ ἀρχίζει διὰ να
    κλέγει.
Θεὸν αὐτὸν ὁπόβρικες, λάτρευε καὶ προσκύνα, 50
στὰ εἴδωλα κεῖς τὰ γλυπτά, μὴ συγκληθεὶς
    σεκείνα.
Καὶ μὴ δουλέψης εὔκαιρους θεοὺς ὡς ἂν ἐμένα,
διατ' ὅλα τοὺς ἐδούλεψα, ὅλα τάχω χαμένα.
Κατέχεις, καὶ ἄλλος σου ἀδελφὸς ὅλος ἐκατακάη,
ἡ μάνα σου ἀπέθανεν, καὶ μὲν ἡ καρδιά μου
    σφάγη.   55
Μόνον ἐσὺ μ' ἀπόμεινες, τὸ φῶς τῶν ὀμματιῶν μου,
γέρος ἤμε καὶ ἀνήμπορος, καὶ ἔπαρε τὴν ὁδόν
    μου.

So Abram took with him his sire and Lot his
    brother's son,
    And his wife Sarah, with the spoils which he as
        yet had won.
A single company they made and left their native
    land,   60
    Towards Mesopotamia they did draw, a footsore,
        wearied band.

VII. ABRAHAM, SARAH AND THE KING
OF CANAAN (Figs. 11–13).

So Lot, Sarah and Abraham quickly their steeds
    prepared,
    Mesopotamia they did leave, towards Palestine
        they fared.
They reached the promised land, and then did
    pass it through and through,
    Saw that the folk was numerous, but no one's
        face they knew.
So of the manners of these men Abraham next
    enquires,   5
    And learns that lightness much prevails alike
        with sons and sires.
His heart sank low within his breast, with fear he
    was possessed,
    Nigh unto Sarah he did draw and thus his
        thoughts expressed.
'Fair is thy face to look upon and full of beauty
    ripe,
    But I am stricken in my years and of ill-favoured
        type.   10

Καὶ πέρνη τὸν πατέραν του, καὶ Λὼτ τὸν ἀνεψιόν του,
καὶ Σάραν τὴν γυναίκαν του, καὶ πέρνη καὶ τὸ
βιόν του.
Μισεύγουν ἐκ τῆς γῆς Σαράν, ὅλοι περμαζο-
μένοι, 60
καὶ σώνουν εἰς τὴν Μεσοποταμία, ὅλοι τους
κουρασμένοι.

VII

Ὁ Λὼτ κ' ἡ Σάρα καὶ Ἀυραὰμ γοργὸν καβαλ-
λικεύγουν,
ἀφίνουν Μεσοποταμιάν, στὴν Παλαιστίνην
ὀδεύουν.
Σόνουν στὴν γῆν τῆς ἐπαγγελίας, καὶ αὐτίνην
τριγυρίζουν,
θοροῦσιν τὸν πολὺ λαόν, κανέναν δὲν γνωρίζουν.
Στρέφετε, ὑλέπη ὁ Ἀυραὰμ αὐτοὺς τοὺς Χανα-
ναίους, 5
κ' ἦτον μεγάλη ἀσυστασιὰ στὰ τέκνα κεῖς
γονέους.
Μέσα ψυχή του ἐδείλιασεν, φόβον παραλαμβάνη,
καὶ πρὸς τὴν Σάραν ἐσήμοσεν, ἄκου τί ἀναθηβάνη.
Ἐσύσε ἄσπρι στὸ πρόσωπον, στὴν ὀμορφιὰν
πορία,
καὶ γώμε γέρος σὰν θωρής, ἄσκημος στὴν
θωρία. 10

I fear they may on thee lay hands and slay me for
thy sake.'
Said Sarah 'listen to my plan lest they thy life
do take.
If they should ask thee, say I am thy sister, not
thy wife;
And this deception practise we only to save thy
life.'
Now when the Canaanites caught view of this new-
entered band,   15
Around the strangers in a crowd all curious
they stand.
They asked them of their native land, their
customs and their race,
And of the purpose which had drawn them unto
that far place.
Abraham thus did answer make: 'Chaldean is our
band:
Fortune it is which us hath sent to sojourn in
this land.'   20
Next they did ask: 'Is this thy wife that thou
dost bring with thee?'
'Nay' answered Abraham in fear, 'my sister ye
do see.'
One Herod at that time was king and lord of all
that place,
Sprung from the progeny of Ham, of Canaan-
itish race.
So they these travellers did lead before his royal
seat,   25
And asked him what his pleasure was, how they
should Sarah treat.

Φονοῦμε μὴ σαρπάξουσιν, κ' ἐμέναν νὰ σκοτόσου·
λέγει του Σάρα, κάτεχε, ἂν θὲς νὰ σὲ γλυτόσουν.
'Ανὲν καὶ σὲ ῥωτήξουσιν, λέγε κῆμε ἀδελφή σου,
καὶ αὐτοῦνον θέλωμεν τοὺς εἰπεῖν, μόνον διὰ νὰ
σαφίσουν.
Κ' οἱ Χαναναῖοι υλέπουσιν τὴν φαμιλιὰν τὴν
ξένην,   15
κέμπηκεν ἠστὸν τόπον τους, ἔτι συνεπαρμένη.
Καὶ αὐτούνους ἐρωτήσασιν τὴν χάριν καὶ τὸν
τρόπον,
καὶ πιὰ φορμὴ σᾶς ἔφερεν στὸν ἐδικόν μας
τόπον.
Καὶ λέγει τους ὁ 'Αβραάμ, ἐκ τῶν Χαλδαίων μέρη
ἡ τύχη μας ἐθέλησεν ἐδὼ διὰ νὰ μᾶς φέρη.   20
Καὶ διὰ τὴν Σάρραν τούπασιν ἀνὲν κένε γυνή του,
καὶ ἀπὸ τὸν φόνον λέγει τους, ὁ κένε ἀδελφή του.
῞Ητον 'Ευρώδης βασιλεὺς καὶ κύριος τοῦ Χεττέος,
ἀπὸ τ' ἀπόγωνα τοῦ Χάμ, ἤτονε χανανέος.
Λοιπὸν ἐκαταδώκαν τους στὸν βασιλέα ὀμπρός
του,   25
καὶ διὰ τὴν Σάρραν λέγουν του ἤντανε ὁρισμός
του.

His answer was they should prepare straightway
    the royal bed,
  And that a banquet should be set and Sarah
    thither led.
So towards evening the thralls the banquet ready
    made,
  And after that upon the couch Sarah they duly
    laid.   30
The king sat down to eat and drink, then to his
    chamber went,
  To which erstwhile they had perforce reluctant
    Sarah sent.
And lo! beside her there was seen a youth with
    whetted brand,
  With face ablaze with anger's light he did
    majestic stand.
So tall his frame, his head well nigh reached unto
    the roof-beam,   35
  And from the light diffused around an angel he
    did seem.
The angel then spake unto him (list to what his
    words were),
  He drew anigh the king and by the name of
    God did swear.
'With all the speed thou canst command from
    yonder couch descend,
  Else thee and all thy family I to destruction
    send.   40
Thinkest thou, wretched man, that thou Sarah for
    thine canst claim,
  Thinkest thou holy Abraham by this thy deed
    to shame?'

Αὐτὸς ἐπηλογήθηκεν νὰ στρώσουσιν τὴν κλίνην,
  νὰ κάμουν δεῖπνον ὄμορφον, μαυτίνην διὰ νὰ
  μείνη.
Καὶ πρὸς τὸ υράδιν οἱ δοῦλοι του τὸν δεῖπνον
  ὀρδινιάζου,
  τὴν Σάραν γδίνουν σύντομα, στὸ στρόμανανε-
  βάζου.   30
Καὶ ἀπήτις ἀποδείπνησεν, στὸ στρόμαν ἀνεβέννει,
  ὁποῦ τὴν Σάραν εἴχασι με τὸ στανιὸν βαλμένην.
Καὶ βλέπει πρὸς τὸ πλάγην της νέον ξισπαθομένον,
  τὸ υλέμαν του παράξενον, πολλὰ τὸν θυμο-
  μένο(ν).
Ἐγγίζει τὸ κεφάλην του ἀπάνω στὰ δοκάρια,   35
  ἄγγελος ἦτον με κορμήν, κ᾽ ἐφάνηκεν καθάρια.
Καὶ πρὸς αὐτὸν ὁ ἄγγελος, ἄκου τὸ τί τοῦ λέγει,
  καὶ με θυμὸν σημόνη του, καὶ τὸν Θεὸν τοῦ
  μνέγει.
Γοργὸν κατέβα σύντομα ἀπὸ τὴν κλίνην κάτω,
  τὰ δ᾽ ὄλη σου τὴν φαμελιὰν κ᾽ ἐσέναν βάνω
  κάτω.   40
Τορμὰς ἐσὺ ταλέπωρε τὴν Σάραν διὰ νὰ πιάσης;
  τὸν Ἀυραὰμ τὸν δίκαιον βούλεσε ν᾽ ἀντρο-
  πιάσης;

M   4

The king was seized with utter fear, from off the
    bed he leapt,
    And Sarah filled with joyfulness at her deliver-
    ance wept.
Straightway the king did give command, and
    Abraham they brought, 45
    And with great awe and reverence to take his
    hand he sought.
'Sir, tell me of the very truth, who is this lady
    fair,
    Whom erstwhile I my thralls did bid unto my
    couch to bear?
Tell me, whence com'st thou, who art thou, and
    what thy journey's need?
    What purpose, drawing thee from home, to
    Palestine did lead?' 50
He answered: 'Abraham am I, from the Chaldean
    land,
    All secretly we did set forth from thence, I and
    my band.
As thou beholdest I am come together with my
    wife:
    This lady whom thou see'st was given as partner
    of my life.
That she my sister was I said through dread and
    fear of thee, 55
    But now I tell thee of a truth she married is to
    me.
I am descendant of that Shem who did this land
    receive,
    Noah his father unto him all Palestine did
    leave.

Καὶ ἀπὸ τὸν φόνον ἔπεσεν ἀπάνω ἐκ τὸ κλινάριν,
κ' ἡ Σάρα ἐχάρικεν πολλὰ πὸς ἧυρεν τόσιν χάριν.

Κ' εἰς μιὸν τοὺς δούλους του ὅρισεν, τὸν Ἀυραὰμ
τοῦ φέραν, 45
καὶ μὲ μεγάλην εὐλάβειαν πιάνη τον ἀκ τὸ
χέρι.

Ἄνθρωπε πέ μου τὸ ἀληθές, τίσονε αὐτῆ γυναίκα,
ὁποῦ ἐπίκα μὲ ὁρισμόν, στὴν κλίνην μου καὶ
θέκαν;

Εἰπέ μου πόθεν καὶ ἀπὸ ποῦ, ποῖος ἧσε καὶ πόθεν
ὁδεύεις

τῆς Παλαιστίνης ἐμπασάν, καὶ τίνε τὸ γυρέ-
βης; 50

Ἦμε ἐγὼ ὁ Ἀυραὰμ ἐκ τῶν Χαλδαίων χώραν,
κουρφὰ ἀπ' αὐτοὺς ἐμίσεψα, ἧτονε τίτια ὥρα.

Καὶ σὰν μας υλέπης ἤρθαμεν ἐδὼ σαυτὰ τὰ μέρη,
καὶ αὐτὴν τὴν ἐθωρὶς ἐδώ, μου δόκασι γιὰ
τέρην.

Μὰ 'γὼ ἀπὸ τὸν φόνον σου ἤλεγα κἔνε ἀδελφή
μου, 55
τόρα σου λέγω κάτεχε ἐμέναν, ἔνε γυνή μου.

Κἦμε ἐκ τὰ πόγονα τοῦ Σὴμ ἀπὸ τὴν Παλαιστίνην,
ὁ Νῶες ὁ πατέρας του εἰς μοίρασιν ταφίνη.

4—2

I came to know the God of heaven, Lord of the
    starry height,
    Who made the sun, moon and the sea, and eke
      the day and night.   60
'Twas He who gave me order strict hither my way
    to make,
    And all the land of Palestine as heritage to
      take.
"For needful is it" (so He said) "thou should'st
    possess that land:
    Thy seed shall grow and multiply in numbers as
      the sand."'
When the king heard what Abraham said, the more
    afraid he grew,   65
    His tongue unto his mouth did cleave, the words
      he spake were few.
'Leave ye this man that with his wife he may take
    rest alone,
    Reverence that chamber where he is as though
      it were his own.'
So to take rest within his room went Abraham
    with his mate,
    And pondering deep the king did go unto his
      room of state.   70
Never at all slept he that night, he lay awake in
    thought,
    He rose at earliest dawn and all his friends
      together brought.
He summoned Abraham unto him and set him in
    a seat,
    With words of deepest reverence he thus his
      guest did greet:

Ἥβρα Θεὸν οὐράνιον, ὁποῦ πίκεν τοὺς ἀστέρες,
ἥλιον, φεγγάριν, θάλασσαν, νύκτες καὶ ταῖς
ἡμέρες.   60
Αὐτὸς ἐμέναν ὅρισεν ἐδῶ νὰ καταντήσω,
τὴν Παλαιστίνην σύντομα νὰ τὴν κλερονομήσω.
Διατ᾽ ἦνε χριαζόμενον νὰ πάρω τὰ καλά σου,
νὰ πληθυνθῇ τὸ σπέρμα μου σὰν ἄμμος τῆς
θαλάσσου.
Καὶ ὡς τ᾽ ἄκουσεν ὁ βασιλεύς, αὐτοῦνον ἐφο-
βήθην,   65
καὶ ποίκεν σχῆμα σιωπῆς, μικρὸν ἐπηλογήθην.
Δότε τ᾽ ἀνδρὸς ἀνάπαυσιν μετὰ τῆς γυναικός του,
καὶ ὁ τόπος ὁποῦ ὁρίζωμεν εὑρίσκεται δικός του.
Κ᾽ ἡ Σάρρα μὲ τὸν Ἀυραὰμ ἐπήγεν καὶ νεπάγη,
καὶ ὁ βασιλεὺς μὲ λογισμὸν ξεχοριστά του
πάγη.   70
Ποσὸς δὲν ἐκοιμήθηκεν, μάλιστα νὰ λογιάζῃ,
σικόνετε πρὸς τὸ ταχύ, καὶ ὅλους τοὺς φίλους
κράζῃ.
Ἐκάλεσεν τὸν Ἀυραάμ, κοντά του τὸν καθίζῃ,
καὶ μὲ μεγάλην εὐλάβειαν λόγια γλυκιὰ τ᾽
ἀρχίζῃ.

'None other god more fearful is than that great
    God of thine,   75
  O Abraham, however thou call'st Him by name
    divine.
Take with thee servants twelve and rams in number
    ten times ten,
  And add to these whatever beasts thou choosest
    from my pen,
That thou unto thy mighty God a sacrifice mayest
    make,
  And pray Him, lest in wrathfulness my life from
    me He take.'   80
He took the beasts and went his way to offer
    sacrifice,
  And there an angel-messenger on this wise gave
    advice.
'Measure thou out this land in all the breadth
    thereof and length,
  So shall thyself and all thy seed be blessed with
    health and strength.
All that spring from thy loins, these too shall like
    thee hold this land,   85
  If only in firm trust in God and piety they
    stand.'
And so when this his sacrifice he had brought to an
    end,
  He turned himself and with the thralls backward
    his way did wend,
To give unto the king those words which God to
    him had told,
  How that by order of the Most High he must
    that country hold.   90

Νομίζω φουερώτατος ἄλλος θεὸς νὰ μὴ ἔνε, 75

ὡσὰν ἐσέναν τ' Ἀβραάμ, καὶ ἀσένε ὅπου ἔνε.

Καὶ ἔπαρε δούλους δώδεκα καὶ κριοὺς κεντηνάρια,

καὶ ἄλλης λοῆς ζωντόνολα ὅσα καὶ ἀθθὲς νὰ

πάρῃς.

Νὰ θυσιάσῃς τὸν Θεὸν τὸν μέγαν μὲ τὴν τάξιν,

νὰ δεηθῆς διαλλόγου μου διὰ νὰ μή με πατάξῃ.

Καὶ πέρνῃ τὸ ζωντόνολον, πάγῃ νὰ θυσιάσῃ, 81

ἄγγελον ἔπεψεν ὁ Θεός, αὐτοῦνον ὀρδινιάζῃ,

Διὰ νὰ μετρήσει αὐτὴν τὴν γῆν, τοῦ μάκρου καὶ

τοῦ πλάτου,

σαυτοῦνον καὶ τὸ σπέρμαν του νὰ πέψῃ τ' ἀγαθά

του.

Αὐτα νὰ παραλάβουσιν ὅσ' εὔγουν ἀπ' ἐσένα, 85

ὅσοι στὴν θεοσέβειαν νάχουσι δουλεμένα.

Καὶ ἀπήτις ἐξετέλειοσεν θυσίαν τὴν καθάρια,

ἐδιάγυρεν τοῦ βασιλεῦ ὅλα τὰ παλλικάρια.

Οσα καὶ ἂν τοῦ πεν ὁ Θεός, ὅλα νὰ τὰ θιβάνη,

καὶ πῶς μὲ ὁρισμὸν Θεοῦ τὴν γῆν παραλαμ-

βάνη. 90

And when the king heard what he said, he rose
　　from off his seat;
　　He took his royal garment off and laid it at
　　　his feet.
His servants he together called and one and all
　　bade pay
　　To Abraham deep reverence where'er he went
　　　his way.
So when the Canaanites did see what thus befell
　　their race,   95
　　How that it was the will of God, they sought
　　　another place.
The king departed from the land their exile too to
　　share,
　　And in his stead did Abraham dwell with all that
　　　with him were.
But, ere he left, to Abraham he gave from out his
　　stocks:
　　Greatly those herds did multiply, greatly increased
　　　those flocks.   100
And many servants too he gave that they these
　　spoils might tend,
　　And strictly charged them their new lord in no
　　　wise to offend.

VIII. HOW ABRAHAM WAS SENT TO
MELCHISEDEK (Figs. 14–17).

Once more God Abraham did bid his saddle-bands
　　to heed,
　　To take clean raiment and choose food fit for his
　　　journey's need:

Τὸ νατακούση ὁ βασιλεύς, ἐπροσικόθηκέν του,
τὸ φόρεμαν τῆς βασιλείας εὔγαλεν κἔδοκέν του.
Καὶ ὅλοι ἐκλήθησαν δοῦλοι του, ἐκείνους διὰ νὰ
ὁρίζη,
ὡς δοῦλοι νὰ τὸν προσκυνοῦν, ὅπου καὶ ἀνε-
γυρίζη.
Καὶ ὡς οἶδαν τὰ γενόμενα οἱ Χαναναίοι ἐφύγα, 95
διατίτον θέλημαν Θεοῦ στοὺς τόπους τους
ἐπήγαν.
Ἐμίσεψεν ὁ βασιλεὺς καὶ πάγη τὴν δουλιάν του,
καὶ Ἀυραὰμ ἐκατοίκησεν μ' ὅλην τὴν φαμιλιάν
του.
Πᾶσα λοῆς ζωντόβολον τοῦ Ἀυραὰμ μοιράζη,
τὸ ἔναν γίνετ' ἑκατόν, τὰ δέκα τοῦ χιλιάζη. 100
Δούλους πολλοὺς ἐπόταξεν, κῆσαν στὸν ὁρισμόν
του,
ἐμπιστεμένα καὶ καλὰ ὑλέπουσιν τὸ δικόν του.

VIII

Καὶ πάλιν ἐλάλησεν ὁ Θεὸς σομαρικὸν νὰ στρώση,
καὶ ροῦχον ἔναν σπαστρικόν, καὶ νὰ βαστὰ
καὶ ὑρῶσιν.

To wit some bread and wine and oil, and also light
    for fire :
  Then tells He him the purpose high to which
    he must aspire.
'Go to the cave that hollowed is in the northern
    mountain-face,   5
  A man thou'lt find that wilder is than any wild
    beast's race.
His nails are of a cubit's length, his beard falls to
    his toe,
  The hair that from his head hangs down right
    to the heel doth go.
Thrice must thou call on him and speak, I charge
    thee for My sake,
  Of unkempt body and eyes wild heed thou must
    never take.   10
Shear thou his nails, shear thou his hair, and raiment
    on him lay,
  Give him to eat, give him to drink, and then his
    blessing pray.
And blessing shalt thou surely have, both thou and
    all thy kind,
  Thy wealth, thy herds, thy family prosperity shall
    find.'
So God commanded : Abraham duly performéd
    all :   15
  He went unto the cave, and there three times
    aloud did call.
'O man of God, come forth,' said he, 'let us
    acquaintance make,
  Let us together counsel hold for God and
    friendship's sake.'

Ἤγουν ψωμὴν καὶ τὸ κρασὶν καὶ λάδιν καὶ φωτία,
καὶ βάνῃ τον εἰς ὁδηγιάν· λέγει του τὴν αἰτία.

Λέγει του νὰ πᾶ στὸ σπήλαιον, στὸ ὄρος τὸ
βορίω· 5
ἄνθρωπος μέσα βρίσκετε, ἄγριος παρὰ θηρίον.

Τὰ νύχια του εἶναι πυχερά, τὰ γένια του ὡς
κάτω,
καὶ τὰ μαλιά του κρέμουνται στὲς πτέρνες του
ἀπὸ κάτω.

Καὶ τρεῖς φωναῖς τοῦ φώναξε, καὶ πέ του ὅγια
μένα
μὴ φοβήθῃς τ᾿ ἄγριον κορμὴν καὶ μάτια ξαγριο-
μένα. 10

Αὐτὸν νυχοτρικούρεψε, τὸ φόρεμαν τοῦ βάλε,
δόστου νὰ φάγῃ καὶ νὰ πγή, καὶ εὐλογίαν λάβε.

Καὶ θέλῃς ἔχειν εὐλογιὰν ἐσὺ καὶ τὰ καλά σου,
στεκάμενα, συρνάμενα, μ᾿ ὅλην τὴν φαμιλιάν
σου.

Καὶ ὅτι τοῦ λέγει ὁ Θεὸς αὐτοῦνος ὀρδινιάζῃ, 15
καὶ πάγῃ πρὸς τὸ σπήλαιον, καὶ τρὶς φωνὲς
φωνάζῃ.

Ἄνθρωπε, λέγει, τοῦ Θεοῦ, ἔλα, νὰ γνωριστοῦμεν,
ἅμα σὰν τ᾿ ὁρίζῃ Κύριος φίλοι νὰ λογιστοῦμεν.

Forth comes the wild Melchisedek, out from the
   cave he creeps:
  His hair hung round about his limbs as shaggy
   as a sheep's.   20
Yet were his words to Abraham full mild and low
   and sweet:
  'What god,' said he, 'hath sent thee here thy
   servant thus to greet?'
And Abraham did answer make: 'The Ruler of
   the sky,
  God the Almighty, on whose truth and faith all
   men rely.
To me he gave the strait command to shear thy
   nails and hair,   25
  And that thou mayest be sustained, bread, oil
   and wine to bear.'
'According to God's gracious word, forthwith so
   let it be:'
  To Abraham he then advanced, bowing with
   courtesy.
He cut his nails, he cut his hair, clothed him in
   raiment meet,
  Kissed and embraced him, and then near himself
   did set his seat.   30
He asked him whence he came and why unto that
   desert spot,
  Why he had lived in exile drear, and why so hard
   his lot.
He answer made: ''Tis forty years since I have
   eaten bread,
  Forty long years have passed away since to this
   spot I fled.

Εὐγήκεν ὁ Μελχισεδέκ, ὅλος ἐξαγριωμένος,
   καὶ τὰ μαλιὰ σὰν πρόβατον ἤτονε φορεμένος. 20
Ἐμίλησεν τοῦ Ἀβραὰμ ἤμερα μετὰ τάξις·
   καὶ πιὸς Θεὸς σ' ἀπέστειλεν ἐμέναν διὰ νὰ
   κράξης;
Καὶ ἀπολογήθην Ἀβραάμ· τοῦ οὐρανοῦ ὁ Κτίστης,
   Θεὸς ὁ παντοκράτωρας, καὶ τῆς ἀληθινῆς τῆς
   πίστης.
Ἐμέναν ἐπαράγγειλεν να σε νυχοτριχοκουρέψω, 25
   καὶ μὲ ψωμὶν καὶ μὲ κρασὶν καὶ λάδιν νὰ σὲ
   θρέψω.
Ἅμαν ἀντόρίζη ὁ Κύριος σύντομα αὐτὸ ἀς γένη·
   καὶ κλίνη τὸ κεφάλην του, στὸν Ἀβραὰμ πηγένη.
Νυχοτριχοκοπίζη τον, τὸ ροῦχον του στολίζει·
   φιλά, περιλαμβάνη τον, κοντά του τὸν καθίζη.
Λέγει του, πόθεν καὶ ἀπὸ ποῦ ἦρθες σ' αὐτὸν τὸν
   τόπον; 31
   ρωτά τον διὰ τὴν ἐγδημιάν, τῆς ἄσκησις τὸν
   κόπον.
Καὶ αὐτὸς ἐπηλογήθηκεν· σαράντα χρόνους ἔχω,
   ἀπὸ τὸ φάγην τοῦ ψωμίου καὶ ἀπὲ τὸν κόσμον
   ἀπέχω.

Water and herbage of the field my sustenance
    supplied,   35
  So scant that sustenance that oft methought I
    should have died.
My father was Iasedek, a man of kingly
    state,
  My mother Salem they did give to be his royal
    mate.
She from the line of Nevron came who Babylon
    did found,
  A kingly race, but one and all to idolatry were
    bound.   40
And in the process of due time two sons unto
    them came,
  Sedek the elder-born and I whom men do Melchi
    name.
One day my father gave command that I should
    fetch some sheep,
  That he unto his heathen gods a sacrifice might
    keep.
With the first break of morning light while still
    the stars shone bright   45
  I did set forth; as yet the moon flooded the
    earth with light.
A thought came o'er my mind—"that moon is
    guided by God's hand,
  'Tis He who with His governance rules sky and
    sea and land."
Straightway this pondering of my soul my footsteps
    backward brought,
  I sought my sire, and without stint unbosomed
    all my thought.   50

Μόνον μὲ χόρτον καὶ νερὸν διαβάζω τὴν ζωήν
μου,   35
καὶ μετ' αὐτὸν παρὰ μικρὸν διαβάζω τὴν πνοήν
μου.

Ἰασεδὲκ καὶ βασιλεὺς τὸν κύριν μου ὀνομάζουν,
καὶ τὴν μητέραν μου Σαλὴμ τὸ ὄνομάν της
κράζουν.

Ἐκ τοῦ Νευρώδι τὰ πώγωνα, αὐτοίνοι ὁποῦ κρα-
τοῦσα,   39
ἀπόκτισεν τὴν Βαβυλών, ἀμὲ εἰδωλολατροῦσα.

Εἶχαν καὶ πρῶτον ἀδελφόν, Σεδὲκ τὸν ἐφωνάζαν,
Μέλχη ἐμὲν τὸν δεύτερον οἱ πάντες ὀνομάζαν.

Κ' ἔδοξεν τοῦ πατέρα μου ἐμέναν διὰ νὰ πέψῃ,
διὰ νὰ τοῦ φέρω πρόβατα, νὰ τὰ εἰδωλολατρέψῃ.

Αὐγήτζαν ἐσυκόθηκα κ' ἦτον ξαστερωμένα,   45
καὶ τὸ φεγγάριν ἔφεγγεν ὡς ἂν ξημερομένα.

Μέσα σ' ἐμὲν ἐλόγιασα, αὐτὰ Θεὸς ὁδεύει,
θάλασσαν, γήν, καὶ οὐρανὸν αὐτοῦνος ἀφεντεύει.

Καὶ ἀπῆτις τούτα λόγιασα, στὸν κήριν μου διαγέρνω,   49
τὰ λόγια σὰν καταλεφτὰ ὅλα του τ' ἀναφέρνω.

"If thou, my father, those poor sheep to sacrifice art fain
    To soulless idols, then know well thou'lt sacrifice in vain.
Nay rather, let us sacrifice to the great God of truth,
    Who dwelleth in the highest heaven, whose every word is sooth.
Those heavens spread above, that sea, this earth on which we stand   55
    Submit unto His government: we rule by His command."
The king thereat was sore displeased, these words he could not brook:
    He started up from off his throne, his voice with passion shook.
He swore to me a mighty oath I should be led away
    And offered as a sacrifice unto his gods of clay.   60
"Me hast thou counselled I should leave the gods whom I adore,
    That I should henceforth worship pay to a god whom I abhor?
They in their anger will arise and drown me in the sea,
    Or else in battle will destroy before mine enemy."
And on a sudden he commands, his words with passion ring,   65
    That I should go to Galilee and sheep therefrom should bring,

Λέγω του, διὰ τὰ πρόβατα, τὰ θὲς νὰ θυσιάσῃς
εἰς τ᾽ ἄψυχα τὰ εἴδωλα, ὅλα τὰ θέλῃς χάσῃ.
Καὶ αὐτοῦν᾽ ἀς θυσιάσωμεν εἰς τὸν Θεὸν καὶ
Κτίστην,
ὁποῦ στὰ ὕψει κατοικᾷ, καὶ θὲ μᾶς δώσει πίστην.
Θάλασσαν, γῆν καὶ οὐρανὸν κ᾽ ἡ γῆς ὁποῦ πατοῦ-
μεν,   55
σαυτοῦνον ὑποτάσσονται, μ᾽ αὐτοῦνον ἀς κρα-
τοῦμεν.
Καὶ ὡς τ᾽ ὄκουσεν ὁ βασιλεύς, πολλὰ βαρυθυ-
μόθην,
καὶ γέμοσεν τὴν μάνηταν, κτὸν θρόνον ἐσικό-
θην.
Καὶ ὀμνύει μου στὰ εἴδωλα ἐμένα διὰ νὰ πιάσῃ
εἰς τοὺς θεοὺς ἀπόλωνα ὀγιὰ νὰ θυσιάσῃ.   60
Ἐμέναν ἐβουλεύτηκες ξένον ἐσὺ νὰ κάμῃς
εἰς τοὺς θεοὺς τοὺς σέβομε, μ᾽ ἄλλον θεὸν μὲ
βάνῃς;
Καὶ θέλουν μου προσοργισθήν, νὰ μὲ καταπον-
τίσουν,
καὶ οἱ ἐχθροὶ στὸν πόλεμον ἐμένα νὰ φανίσουν.
Κεὶς μιὸν κάμνη ὁρισμὸν μόλην του τὴν μαλαία,
νὰ πᾶ νὰ φέρω πρόβατα ἀπὸ τὴν Γαλιλαία.   66
M   5

To offer them a sacrifice to the gods to whom he
    clave,
    Lest in their anger they arise and sink him
        'neath the wave.
All fasting as I was I turned my steps towards
    Galilee :
    No morsel had I in my scrip of food to strengthen
        me.   70
Another order too he gave—that those who loved
    his race
    Together should their children bring unto the
        selfsame place,
That these a sacrifice should be and share my
    dreadful fate :
    Obediently they gather them and my return
        await.
But when my mother heard that word and learned
    of the device,   75
    That they and I together were a destined
        sacrifice,
She bade my brother there and then from home to
    fly apace
    And give me warning to depart unto another
        place,
In hope perchance I might thereby my angry father
    shun,
    And by a hairsbreadth in my flight pursuing
        doom outrun.   80
Unto my brother did I give my clothes, told him
    to keep
    These, and to hand them to my sire together
        with the sheep.

Νὰ θυσιάσῃ στοὺς θεοὺς διὰ νὰ τὸν ἀγαποῦσι,
  για νὰ μὴν τοῦ προσοργισθοῦν, νὰ τὸν καταπον-
  τίσουν.
Καὶ νηστικὸς ἐμίσεψα στὴν Γαλιλαίαν νὰ πάγω,
  καὶ δὲν ἐβάστουν μετὰ μὲν τίβοτες διὰ νὰ
  φάγω.   70
Κ' ἔκαμεν μέγαν ὁρισμὸν ὅλοι νὰ μαζοκτοῦσι,
  νὰ φέρουσιν τὰ τέκνα τους, ὅσοι τὸν ἀγαποῦσι.
Νὰ θυσιάσουσιν αὐτὰ ἀντάμα μεταμένα,
  σύντομα τὰ μαζόξασιν κ' ἐμέναν ἀναμένα.
Καὶ ὡς ἔμαθεν τὸν ὁρισμὸν ἡ ἐδική μου μάνα, 75
  τὰ βρέφοι πῶς μαζόνουσιν κ' ἐμέναν ἐθηβάναν.
Καὶ μὲ σπουδὴν καὶ ξεδρομὴν πέμπῃ τὸν ἀδελφόν
  μου
  μηνόντα ὅσον ἠμπορῶ νὰ διαβῶ σἄλλον
  δρόμον.
Ὀγιὰ νὰ λύψω κτὸν θυμὸν τὸν μέγαν τοῦ κυροῦ
  μου,
  εἴτις κ' ἐγὼ παρὰ μικρὸν καμπόσον ἐντηροῦ-
  μου.   80
Λοιπὸν τὰ ρούχα μου ἐγδήθηκα, πέμπω τα τοῦ
  κυροῦ μου,
  ἀμάδιν με τὰ πρόβατα· δίδο τα τ' ἀδελφοῦ
  μου.

He took all these and bent his road to Salem,
　　sadly I
　　To gain the mount called Olivet with faltering
　　　　steps did try.
Such was the name I gave the hill, for there I hoped
　　to find　　　　　　　　　　　　　　　　　　85
　　Mercy in place of father's wrath and sacrifice
　　　　unkind.
Before my face there stood the folk all overcome
　　with fears
　　And full of angry thoughts because they saw
　　　　their children's tears.
I lifted up mine eyes and sought to find out
　　heaven's gate:
　　The prayer I uttered unto God I now to you
　　　　relate.　　　　　　　　　　　　　　　　　90
I said: "O God of heaven and earth and Lord of
　　the wide sea,
　　Let all this land be overwhelmed with all that
　　　　therein be,
Let all their gods and idols fall in grip of doom
　　held fast,
　　Let all that to them homage pay into the abyss
　　　　be cast."
In a few words I will describe what to that folk
　　befell—　　　　　　　　　　　　　　　　　　95
　　God heaved the earth with mighty shock and
　　　　sent them down to hell.
Now when I saw that awesome sight, the doom of
　　humankind,
　　That not a man and not a babe did there remain
　　　　behind,

Φορτόνη, σύρνη, πάγη τα εἰς τὴν Σαλήμ, καὶ
   μόνος
ἐγὼ ἄντικρυς ἐπέρασα εἰς τὸ ὄρος τοῦ Ἐλαιῶ-
   νος.
Αὐτὸν ἐπ' ὀνομάτησα διανάβρω ἐλεμοσύνη   85
   κεῖς τὸν θυμὸν τοῦ βασιλέως κεῖς στὴν ἀσπλαγχ-
   νοσύνην.
Ὅιτον ἄντικρυς μου ὁ λαὸς στὴν χώραν ὀργισμέ-
   νος,
καὶ ἀπὸ τὸ κλάμαν τῶν παιδιῶν ἤτονε συγχησ-
   μένος.
Τὰμμάτια μου ἀντράνισαν στὸν οὐρανὸν ἀπάνω,
καὶ τὰ ἐπαρακάλεσα τόρα ταναθηβάνω.   90
Εἶπα, Θεὲ τοῦ οὐρανοῦ, τῆς γῆς καὶ τῆς θαλάσσης,
ἡ χώρα ἀς καταποντιστή, μ' ὅλους νὰ τὴν
   χαλάσης,
Καὶ οἱ θεοὶ καὶ εἴδωλα ὅλοι νὰ κρεμνηστοῦσι,
   καὶ ὅσοι αὐτάνα σέβουνται μαυτοὺς νὰ βιθυσ-
   τοῦσι.
Τὸ εἰπεῖν τὸν λόγον σύντομα, μέγας σεισμὸς
   ἀρχίζει,   95
   τὴν χώραν μὲ ὅλον τὸν λαὸν ὁ Θεὸς καταποντί-
   ζει.
Καὶ ὡς οἶδα τὸ παράξενον θαύμασμαν ὁποῦ
   γίνην,
   καὶ δὲν ἐγλύτωσεν ἄνθρωπος ἢ υρέφος ναπο-
   μείνη,

How they were overwhelmed and all were swallowed
    in earth's wave,
     I pondered deep within my heart and fled unto
      this cave.   100
Forty full years have passed away, never a man I've
    seen,
     None, saving thou, O Abraham, has nigh this
      cavern been.'
So spake Melchisedek, and then Abraham a table
    spread,
     That they together might break fast he set out
      wine and bread.
'Nay,' said Melchisedek to him, 'first must I plenty
    take   105
     From out thy store that I to God a sacrifice may
      make.'
First with the oil he bathed the rock, the loaves in
    order laid,
     Then with outpouring of the wine he a libation
      made.
And when the sacrifice was o'er, their hands in
    prayer they raise,
     And after that they ate and drank, and sang a
      hymn of praise.   110
He promiséd Melchisedek a thank-offering to
    bring,
     A tenth of all his house possessed to proffer to
      his King.
Then Abraham went to his home, and thanks to
    God did pay,
     That he had brought a fellowman to trust in
      Him that day.

Μᾶλλον ἡ γῆ κατάπιεν τους καὶ καταποντισ-
τίκα,

σὲ μέναν ἦρτεν λογισμός, κ' ἐδῶ στὸ σπήλαιον
ἐμπίκα. 100

Σαράντα χρόνους ἔκαμα, καὶ ἄνθρωπος δὲν ἐφάνη,
μόνον αὐτὸν τὸ πρόσωπον, ἐσέναν τ' 'Αυραάμι.

Καὶ ἀπ' εἴτι ἀποσύντιχεν, οἰκονομὰ νὰ πιάση
ὁ 'Αυραὰμ ψωμήν, κρασίν, ὁμάδι διὰ νὰ φάσιν.

"Οχι τοῦ λέγει ὁ Μελχισεδέκ, ὁμπρὸς θέλω νὰ
πιάσω 105

μύρια ἐκ τὰ φερνάμενα, ὁγιὰ νὰ θυσιάσω.

Τὴν πέτραν λάδιν ἔλειψεν, τοὺς ἄρτους ἐτοιμάζη,
καὶ μὲ κρασὶν ὁ Μελχισεδὲκ τὸν Κύριον
θυσιάζη.

Καὶ ἀπίτης ἐθυσίασεν, ὁμάδι προσκυνοῦσι,
καὶ τότες τρῶν καὶ πίννουσιν, καὶ τὸν Θεὸν
ὑμνοῦσι. 110

"Εταξεν τοῦ Μελχισεδὲκ νὰ φέρνη εὐχαριστεία,
ἐκ τὰ καλὰ τοῦ οἴκου του νὰ δίδη δεκατία.

'Εδιάγυρεν ὁ 'Αυραὰμ καὶ δόξαζεν τὸν Κτίστην,
τὸ πῶς εὑρέθην ἄνθρωπος καὶ ἔχει Θεὸν στὴν
πίστην.

Nor yet did Abraham at home his promised gift
    forget,   115
  As present to the Lord a tenth from all aside he
    set.
Again he journeyed to the cave, the offering with
    him bore,
  And for his gift, as each day passed, was blesséd
    more and more.

IX. ABRAHAM ENTERTAINS THE THREE YOUNG
    TRAVELLERS.   MIRACLE OF THE CALF
    (Figs. 18, 19).

And making his abode he pitched his tents on
    Mamre's plain,
  And there with liberality strangers did enter-
    tain.
With heart hospitable and kind there he kept open
    board,
  And unto every passer by a welcome did accord.
He set before them meat and drink, washed them
    from travel's stain: 5
  A bed he furnished that the night resting they
    could remain.
But, since he hated all things good, the Devil
    closed the ways,
  For envy towards the wayfarer he felt since
    Adam's days.
All hungrily did Abraham await the longed for
    guest,
  Three days and nights without reward he
    sacrificed his rest.   10

Τὸ τάσιμον τῆς δεκατιᾶς ὁ Ἀυρααμ ἀρχίζῃ,   115
ἐκ τὰ καλὰ τοῦ οἴκου του αὐτοῦνον δεκατίζῃ.
Ἐπήγενεν στὸ σπήλαιον αὐτοῦνα φορτωμένος,
καὶ διάγυρεν καθημερινόν, αὐτὸς εὐλογημένος.

IX

Λοιπὸν αὐτὸς ἐσκήνωσεν εἰς τῆς Μαυρῆς τὸν
    τόπον,
ὁποῦχεν τὴν φιλοξενιὰν καὶ τὸν μεγάλον κόπον.
Φιλοξενίαν καὶ τράπεζαν ὁ Ἀυραάμις στίνη,
    καὶ ὅσοι διαβάτες καὶ ἀν διαβοῦν, ὅλους τοὺς
    ἀναμένη.
Νὰ φάν, νὰ πιοῦσιν μετ᾽ αὐτόν, τὰ πόδια τους νὰ
    πλύνη,   5
    καὶ γιὰ περισσὴν ἀνάπαυσιν, τοὺς ἔστησεν καὶ
    κλίνη.
Καὶ σφάλισεν ὁ μισόκαλος ὁ δαίμονας τὲς στρά-
    τες,
    καὶ διὰ τὸν φθόνον τοῦ Ἀδὰμ ζηλόνη τοὺς
    διαβάτες.
Καὶ νηστικὸς εἰς τὴν ὁδὸν διαβάτες ἀναμένει,
    τρία μερόνυκτα κάθετον, κανὴς δὲν ἀναφάνη.

And when God saw the toil he had and all his soul's
       deep pain,
   From out the Devil's hinderance to free him
       He was fain.
The third day came and then the Lord proferred a
       welcome sight,
   Father, and Son and Holy Ghost with blessing
       all bedight.
In guise of three young travellers on foot their
       way they plied,   15
   And from afar those travellers Abraham's eyes
       espied.
But when anigh they drew, they turned and went
       another way,
   With haste they passed along their road, it seemed
       they could not stay.
Then Abraham wrung his hands in grief, to them
       aloud he cried:
   'Come ye, and eat and drink with me, all good
       things I'll provide.'   20
Those youths still showed anxiety to pass upon
       their road,
   No need had they of food and drink to visit
       that abode.
To hasten forward on their way indeed was their
       first choice:
   But when they saw his eagerness they hearkened
       to his voice.
So Abraham took them within the shelter of his
       tent,   25
   And for the nonce disconsolate away the Devil
       went.

Καὶ ὡς εἶδεν ὁ Θεὸς τὸν κόπον του καὶ πρῆκαν τὴν
μεγάλη,   11
    καὶ φθονεροῦ τὸ ἐμπόδισμα, βούλετε νὰ τὴν
    εὐγάλη.
Κεῖς τρίτον ἔδειξεν ὁ Θεὸς σχῆμα χαριτωμένον,
    Πατήρ, Υἱός, καὶ Ἅγιον Πνεύμας εὐλογημένο.
Τρὶς νέοι δίχνουν κέρχουνται ὡς ἄνδρες ὁδοι-
πόροι,   15
    τοὺς πιοὺς αὐτοὺς ὁ Ἀυραὰμ ἀπὸ μακρὰς
    ἐθώρει.
Καὶ ἀπήτις ἐσημώσασιν, εἰς ἄλλον δρόμον πένου,
    καὶ μὲ σπουδὴν ἐβιάζουντα, δίχνουν καὶ δ'
    ἀπομένου.
Δέννη τὰ χέρια του ὁ Ἀυραὰμ, αὐτοὺς ἐπαρακάλει
    νὰ πᾶν νὰ φάσιν μετ' αὐτόν, πᾶσα καλὸν
    ναυγάλει.   20
Κ' οἱ νέοι δίχνουν, βιάζουνται τὴν στράταν τους
    νὰ πᾶσι,
    ὀλίγοι χρία τοὺς κάμνουσιν, ἔχουσι διὰ νὰ
    φάσι.
Λοιπὸν οἱ νέοι μὲ σπουδὴν γλήγορα δοιποροῦσα,
    μὰ ὑλέποντας τὴν προθυμιὰ τὴν εἶχεν τὰ πα-
    κοῦσα.
Καὶ πέρνη τους ὁ Ἀυραάμ, καὶ μπένη στὸ καλ-
ήβη·   25
    (κ)αὶ ὁ δαίμονας ὁ φθονερὸς πολλὰ βαρὰ τὸ
    θλίβη.

The host three measures of fine flour took and
    a calf did slay,
    And Sarah butter and new bread before her
    guests did lay.
In cauldron she made water hot that she might
    wash their feet,
    And for the resting of their limbs she strewed
    with rugs a seat.   30
The feasting guests asked Abraham whether he
    had a son,
    And he in answer said to them: 'I have not
    even one.'
Then in return they answer made: 'Know, Abraham,
    the truth,
    Thou in due time a son shalt have: we say it of
    a sooth.'
But Sarah laughed aside and then to them did
    speak these words: 35
    'How can such thing as this be true, my masters
    and my lords?
Barren am I, my husband too with age is all
    fordone:
    Come tell me, how can such as we be blesséd with
    a son?'
They turned and spake to Abraham: 'Yet shall a
    son be born,
    And through the path of life that son shall every
    grace adorn.'   40
To Sarah said they: 'Though thy heart in unbelief
    is cold,
    By sign we undertake to vouch the truth of what
    we've told.'

Τρι' ἀμέτρα σιμηδόλαδον, καὶ τὸ μοσχάρι σφάζῃ,
νότυρον καὶ ζεστὰ ψομιὰ ἡ Σάρα ἑτοιμάζῃ.
Καὶ ζέστανεν καὶ τὸ νερόν, τὰ πόδια τους νὰ
πλύνῃ,
καὶ τοίμασεν ἀνάπαυσιν, καὶ στρώνῃ τους τὴν
κλίνη. 30
Τρόγοντας λέσιν τἀυραάμ, υἱὸν αὐτὸς ἀνέχῃ,
καὶ ἀπηλογήθην κεῖπεν τους, οὐδὲ ποσὸς μετέχῃ.
Καὶ πάλιν ξαναλέσιν του, ἤξευρε, 'Αβραάμι,
τοῦτον ἀσίσε θαρετός, υἱὸν ἐσὺ θὲς κάμι.
'Η Σάρα παραγέλασε καὶ πρὸς αὐτοὺς ὁμίλει, 35
πῶς ἔνε τοῦτον ἐμπορετόν, ἀφέντες μου καὶ
φίλοι;
Στῆρα καὶ γρέα βρίσκομαι, καὶ ἄντρας μου
γεροντάκη,
πῶς ἔνε μπορεζάμενον νὰ κάμωμεν παιδάκι;
Καὶ πάλε ξαναλέγουν του· νάνε νεβαιωμένος,
μέλλη του υἱὸς νὰ γεννηθὴ πολλὰ χαριτω-
μένος. 40
'Η Σάρα, λέγω, δυσπιστά, ἀμήν, ἀμήν σοι λέγω,
ἀλήθια λέγω, κάτεχε εἰς ὅτι καὶ ἀσοῦ μνέγω.

The mother of that little calf around she wandered
    lone,
    In sorrow for her lost offspring she made inces-
        sant moan.
But when those youthful travellers had risen to
    their feet,   45
    That calf rose too and gambolling did run its dam
    to meet.

X. THE ASSAULT UPON LOT'S HOUSE. THE
    MIRACLE OF THE FLAME. THE DESTRUCTION
    OF SODOM AND GOMORRAH (Figs. 20, 21).

Meanwhile those youths towards Sodom and
    Gomorrah took their way,
    And there arriving went within the house of Lot
    to stay.
But in their lust the Sodomites after the youths did
    burn,
    Well in their eagerness they mark the house to
    which they turn.
So when night fell they congregate and a loud
    knocking make   5
    At Lot's door, crying: 'Open there, we fain
    those youths would take.'
But Lot made answer: 'Daughters twain I have
    within my door,
    Fair are they and as white as stars that glitter in
    heaven's floor:
These, that ye may do unto them e'en as ye list,
    retain,
    But from these strangers who are guests ye must
    your hands refrain.'   10

Ἡ δάμαλις τοῦ μοσχαρίου ἡ μάνα τὸ γυρεύη,
    ἔξω καὶ μέσα ὅδελέγοντας διατὸ μουσκάρι
    ὁδεύη.
Καὶ ἀπήτις ἐσυκόθησαν οἱ νέοι ἐκ τὸ τραπέζη,   45
    ὁ μόσχος ἐνεστάθηκεν, καὶ τριπηδὸ καὶ τρέχη.

X

Κ᾽ οἱ νέοι πρὸς τὰ Σόδομα καὶ Γόμαρα παγένουν,
    στὸ σπίτην κ᾽ εἰς τὴν κατοικιὰν τοῦ Λὼτ αὐτοὶ
    ἐμπένου.
Κ᾽ οἱ γέροντες οἱ πονηροὶ στοὺς νέους ἐλιξέψα,
    καὶ μὲ μεγάλην ξεδρομιὰ στοχάζουντε ποῦ
    γνέψα.
Καὶ αὐτοίνοι περμαζόνουντε, τὴν νύκτα κατα-
    κροῦσι,   5
    τοῦ Λὼτ λέγουσιν, ἄνοιξε· τοὺς νέους τοῦ
    ζητοῦσι.
Καὶ ὁ Λὼτ ἐπηλογήθηκεν, τὲς δύο μου θυγατέρες,
    ἀποῦνε ἄσπρες καὶ ὄμορφες σὰν τ᾽ οὐρανοῦ
    ἀστέρες,
Ἐπάρετε καὶ κάμετε μ᾽ αὐταῖς τὸ θέλημά σας,
    καὶ ἀπὸ τοὺς ξένους λοίπεται, πιένετε ἀνάθεμά
    σας.   10

But straight the eldest of the youths cried unto
    Lot: 'Be bold,
  Open the door, for I with them am fain to
    converse hold.'
The door, till then so strongly barred, he forthwith
    opened wide,
  A mighty sheet of scorching flame shot from
    within outside:
That flame encompassed them around, and back-
    wards they did fall,   15
  Not from repentance, but because the heat did
    them appal.
When Lot that marvel did behold, low on his
    knees he fell,
  He bowed his head down to the ground, be-
    seeching them to tell
Whence with such mightiness of power they came
    unto that place:
  'I am your servant, Ye my Lords, grant me
    I pray your grace.'   20
'With all the speed thou canst command,' said they,
    'hie thee away,
  Thou and thy family, for here ye may no longer
    stay.
Unto this town we now have come, a place by
    God accursed,
  Unto this folk of wickedness in flood of sins
    immersed,
That each and every one alike we may to doom
    send down,   25
  Men, women, children—and in gulf of hell's
    abyss may drown.

Καὶ ὁ εἶς ἀπὸ τοὺς τρεῖς ἐπιλογήθηκεν ὁ πρῶτος,
παράνοιξε τὴν πόρταν σου, νὰ τοὺς μιλήσω
πρόστος.
Λοιπὸν τὴν πόρταν ἤνοιξεν, ὁποῦτον σφαλισμένη,
φλόγα πολλὴ ἀπὸ φωτιὰς ἤτονε προβαλμένη.
Κ' ἡ φλόγα τοὺς ἐσβόλωσεν, καὶ ὀμπρὸς ὀπίσω
ἐππέσα,   15
καὶ οὐδὲ ποσὸς μετανοοῦν εἰς ὅσα καὶ ἀνευτέσα.
Καὶ ὡς εἶδεν ὁ Λὼτ τὸ θαύμασμαν, ὀμπρός τους
γονατίζη,
καὶ κλίνει τὸ κεφάλην του, κάτω στὴν γῆν
τογγίζη.
Πγῆστε καὶ πόθεν ἤρτεται σεμὲν τὰ δυναμάρη,
στὸν δοῦλον σας ἀφέντες μου, κἔχετε τόσιν
χάρη;   20
Ὅσον πορὶς τοῦ λέγουσιν, μόλην τὴν φαμιλιάν
σου,
ἔπαρε τόρα μετὰ σέ, πάγενε τὴν δουλιάν σου.
Σταῖς χώρες τούταις ἤρθαμεν καὶ τόπον ὀργισ-
μένον,
σαυτὸν τὸν πονηρὸν λαὸν καὶ τὸν κριματισ-
μένον.
Καὶ ὅλους ἐτούτους θέλομεν νὰ καταποντιστοῦσι,
ἄνδρες, γυναῖκες καὶ πεδιά, ὅλα νὰ βιθησ-
τοῦσιν.   26

M   6

Haste thee with speed from hence and take with
    thee what thou canst find,
  Let none of all thy family lingering remain
    behind.
No matter what the sounds ye hear, turn not the
    cause to see,
  For whoso turns to look behind pillar of salt
    shall be.'   30
His saddle-bags he laded full with oil and wine
    and bread,
  And with him on his way his wife and his two
    daughters led.
Away from the doomed town he drew, and entering
    in a dale
  Passed towards the hill of Sigor which did lie
    beyond that vale.
Now mighty rumblings of earthquake in Sodom's
    parts did boom,   35
  And thunder-claps exceeding loud, the har-
    bingers of doom.
A sulphurous welter of black pitch the abyss
    belched forth in ire,
  And from the heavens down did rain a hail of
    blazing fire.
Above, below and all around was heard destruction's
    knell,
  As Sodom, upheaved from its roots, went hurt-
    ling down to hell.   40
And cities four and all they held in burning ashes
    sank,
  Due punishment of lawlessness and of offences
    rank.

Καὶ συνεσπούδαξε γοργόν, ἐσοὶ κ'ἡ φαμιλοιά σου,
καὶ ἔπαρε σὺ τὸ ἔχει σου, πάγενε τὴν δουλιάν
σου.
Κ' εἰς ὅτι καὶ ἀνακούσετε, μηδὲν στραφῆτε ὀπίσω,
καὶ ὅπιος ἐκεῖνος θέλῃ στραφήν, στύληαλὸς νὰ
πίσω.   30
Φορτόνη τα τὸ σωμαρικά, κρασίν, ψωμὶν καὶ λάδιν,
πέρνη τὲς θυγατέρες του καὶ τὴν γυναῖκαν του
ὀμάδιν.
Λοιπὸν αὐτὸς ἐμίσεψεν καὶ πάγη τὴν δουλιάν του,
καὶ μετ' αὐτὸν ἔσυρνεν καὶ αὐτὴν τὴν φαμιλιάν
του.
Καὶ ἀπίτης ἐπομάκρυνεν, ἐμπένη εἰς μονοπάτην,   35
σ' ὄρος Σιγὼρ καλούμενον, εἰς ἔναν λαγκαδάκιν.
Συσμοὶ μεγάλοι γίνουνται στὰ Σώδομα καὶ
κτύποι,
βροντὲς μεγάλαις, ταραχές, τῆς βουλησὰς οἱ
κτύποι.
Ἡ ἄβυσσος ἐξέρασεν πίσσανακατωμένην,
καὶ πύριν υρέχει οὐρανὸς μεστίαν αὐτουμένην.
Καὶ σύγκλησις ἐγύνετο ἀπάνω καὶ ἀπὸ κάτω,   41
στὰ Σώδομα πρὸς τὸν βυθὸν ἐγύραν ἄνω κάτω.
Καὶ χώρες ἐβολήσασιν τέσσερις μὲ τοὺς ἀνθρώ-
πους,
κτὲς ἀνομίες ταῖς πολλὲς καὶ τοὺς κακοὺς τοὺς
τρόπους.

But when the wife of Lot did hear those dreadful
    thunderings,
    Knowing the meaning of the sound, that it
      destruction brings,
She for her country and her folk full sorely was
    distrest,   45
    And looking back on that dread sight with
      anguish beat her breast.
Sudden her frame was changed to salt, and she all
    rigid grew,
    The living colour of her face turned to a parch-
      ment hue.

XI. THE PURIFICATION OF LOT (Figs. 22, 23).

Lot and his daughters on the mount did a new
    dwelling make,
    Those daughters there between themselves did
      a strange counsel take.
With wine they made their father drunk: each to
    the other said,
    'The world is now quite overthrown, all other
      men are dead;
Let us twain with our father lie, and thereby raise
    new seed,   5
    So in the process of due time mankind afresh
      shall breed.'
The elder lay with him the first, the old man nought
    perceived,
    And then the second in her turn, and by him
      both conceived.

Καὶ ὡς τἄκουσεν τοὺς υροντισμοὺς τοῦ Λώτου ἡ
   γενέκα, 45
σαυτὴν τὴν καταπόντησιν στὲς χώρες ὁποῦ
   θέκα,
Διὰ τὴν πατρίδα καὶ δυκοὺς πολλὰ πικρὰ λυπήθην,
καὶ στράφην κεῖδεν τὸν θυμὸν καὶ δέρνετον
   στὰ στήθη.
Κ' εἰς μιὸν ἀπολιθώθηκεν καὶ γίνετον ἀλατζένη,
καὶ καταστάθην ἡ ὄψι της ὡσὰν καναβιτζένη. 50

XI

Καὶ ὁ Λὼτ κ' ἡ θυγατέρες του στὸ ὅρος κατοι-
   κοῦσιν,
καὶ αὐτοῦναις συμβουλεύουντε, τὸν κύριν τους
   μεθοῦσι.
Πιστεύοντας καὶ χάθηκεν ὁ κόσμος με τοὺς ἀνθρώ-
   πους,
αὐτίνες ἐλογιάσασιν εἴτια λογῆς τοὺς τρόπους.
Ἀς θέση ὁ γέρος μεταμάς, σπέρμα διὰ νὰ γένη, 5
ὀλίγον τὸ κατόλιγον ὁ κόσμος νὰ πληθύνη.
Καὶ θέττη πρώτη μετ' αὐτόν, καὶ ὁ γέρος δὲν
   ἐγροίκα,
καὶ τότες θέττη δεύτερη, καὶ ἀντάμα ἐγκαστρο-
   θίκα.

And when Lot knew what had been done, with
    grief his heart did fail:
  He took them both to Abraham and told him
    all the tale.   10
And when that tale of wickedness to Abraham's
    ears was brought,
  How that through drunkenness with wine that
    deed of sin was wrought,
'Now go thy way, my son,' said he, 'unto the
    river Nile,
  Which issueth forth from Paradise, that there
    thou reconcile
Thyself with God; for great the sin that thou
    'gainst Him hast done,   15
  In that through this excess of wine such mockery
    thou hast won.
That evil deed of thine is like the seeds of death
    to plant,
  But since the sin unwitting was, God may thee
    pardon grant.'
So under guidance of God's hand he Nile's waters
    sought,
  And from that stream three brands of wood he
    back to Abraham brought.   20
Cedar and pine and cypress wood did those three
    brands comprise,
  And from that trinity of woods salvation's founts
    arise.
When Abraham saw him back return, great wonder
    filled his heart,
  For he had deemed that by that stream he would
    from life depart.

Καὶ ἀπήτις ἐξεξήνησεν ὁ γέρος τὸ φορέθην,
πέρνη τες, πὰν εἰς τὸν Ἀυραάμ, καὶ ὅλα τα
ξηγορεύθην.   10
Καὶ ὡς ἤκουσεν ὁ Ἀυραὰμ τὴν τόσιν ἀσωτίαν,
ὁποῦ διὰ τὴν μέθην τοῦ κρασιοῦ, ὁποῦτον
ἁμαρτία.
Σήρε νὰ πάγης, τέκνον μου, στὸν ποταμὸν τὸν
Νίλον,
ποῦ εὐγένη ἐκ τὴν παράδεισον, τὸν Θεὸν νὰ
κάμης φίλον.
Διατὶ μέγαν τὸ ἁμάρτημαν αὐτοῦνον ὁποῦ ἐργάσ-
της,   15
καὶ τὸ περισσομέθυσμα σέκαμεν καὶ γελάστης.
Αὐτῆ βουλῆ τοῦ δόθηκεν νὰ κακοθανατήση,
στάμάρτημαν τὸ στανικὸν ὁ Θεὸς νὰ τοῦ συμ-
παθήση.
Καὶ αὐτὸν ἐφύλαξεν ὁ Θεός, στὸν ποταμὸν τὸν
φέρνη,
καὶ τοὺς δαυλοὺς ἐβάσταζεν, στὸν Ἀυραὰμ
γιαγέρνη.   20
Πεύκος καὶ κέδρος, κάτεχε, καὶ αὐτὸν τὸ κυπαρίσση
ἦσαν αὐτάνα τὰ δαυλιά, τῆς σωτηρίας ἡ υρύσις.
Τὸ νὰ τὸν δὴ καὶ Ἀυραάμ, παράξενον τοῦ φάνη,
γιατὶ διαΰτω τὸν ἔπεμψεν, ἐκεῖ διὰ ναποθάνη.

He kissed him, clasped him to his arms, and set for
    him a seat,   25
    And with these words his brother's son on his
        return did greet.
'Now know I, my belovéd son, forgiveness thou
    hast won
    From God for that great sin of thine which thou
        'gainst Him hast done.'
Then the twain went upon their way and reached
    a barren hill,
    And on the side thereof a trench with these three
        brands did fill.   30
In a triangle's form therein those three brands were
    inlaid :
    Thereafter Abraham to Lot further command-
        ment made.
He bade him go his way with speed to the river
    Jordan's strand,
    And from that stream bring water clear to pour
        upon each brand.
'Away there four and twenty miles the river
    Jordan lies,   35
    Now go thy way and hither bring water from its
        supplies.
Daily with water from this source thou must these
    brands bedew,
    Until from out those barren stocks blossoms do
        burst to view.'
So Lot the task which Abraham set obediently
    essayed,
    With water drawn from Jordan's flood those
    brands three months he sprayed.   40

Φιλή, περιλαμβάνη τον, κοντά του τὸν καθίζη, 25

μὲ πρόλογον καὶ συντιχιὰν ἤτια λογῆς τ' ἀρχίζη.

Τόρα γνωρίζω, τέκνον μου, κἔχεις συμπαθημένα

τὰ κρίματά σου ὁ Θεός, τὰ ἔχεις καμομένα.

Πέρνου, μισεύουσιν κ' οἱ δύο, καὶ ὁμάδι συνοδεύου,

κ' εἰσε ψηλὸν ἑρμοχάρακον τὰ ξύλα αὐτὰ

φυτεύου. 30

Κ' εἰς τρίγονον τὰ φύτευσαν αὐτάνα ἔναν τάλλω,

καὶ εἴτι του εἶπεν ὁ Ἀυραὰμ τόρα ταναθιβάνω.

Καὶ λέγει του μετὰ ἐντολῆς στὸν ποταμὸν Ἰορδάνην

νὰ πᾶ νὰ φέρνη τὸ νερόν, στὰ ξύλα νὰ τὸ βάνη.

Λέγει του, εἰκοσιτέσσερα μίλια ἔχει ὁ Ἰορ-

δάνης, 35

νὰ πᾶς νὰ κουβαλῆς νερόν, στὰ ξύλα νὰ τὸ

βάνης.

Κήτια λογῆς καθημερινὸν αὐτοῦνον ὡς τακοῦσι,

ὥστε νὰθθίσουν οἱ δαυλοί, καὶ νὰ περιπλεκ-

τοῦσιν.

Λοιπὸν μὲ μεγάλην προθυμιὰν αὐτὸς ὁ Λὼτ ἀρχίζει,

τρεῖς μῆνες ἐπειράζετον τὰ ξύλα νὰ ποτίζει. 40

And when God saw his willingness of mind and
    all his pain,
    From this the labour of his hands to free him
    He was fain.
Sudden those brands did blossom forth, those
    stocks sent out a shoot,
    Within that rock where they were laid, each now
    had taken root.
When Lot that marvel did behold, great wonder
    filled his soul,   45
    He hied him back to Abraham and told him of
    the whole.
Straight Abraham saddled his steed, and to the
    place did ride,
    With his own eyes he wished to see what did
    those brands betide.
In wonder at that marvellous sight his hands to
    God he raised,
    No service more on Lot he laid, but the Creator
    praised.   50
Those brands do signify for man redemption from
    his sin;
    Thereby shall all the guilt-stained world pardon
    and cleansing win.
Their roots are triple and their crowns likewise do
    part in three,
    But yet their stems, like human frame, in unity
    agree.
When Abraham saw that wickedness pardoned by
    God's good grace,   55
    With satisfaction in his heart he turned him to
    his place.

Καὶ ὡς εἶδεν ὁ Θεὸς τὸν κόπον του καὶ προθυμιὰν
  μεγάλην,
ἀπὸ τὸν κόπον τὸν πολὺν ἐθέλησεν ναυγάλη.
Εἰς μιὸν ἀθισοῦσιν οἱ δαυλοὶ καὶ ῥίκτουν βλαστα-
  ρ(ά)κια,
καθῶς αὐτὸς τζε φύτευσεν μέσα εἰς τὰ χαράκια.
Καὶ ὡς οἶδεν ὁ Λὼτ τὸ θαύμασμαν, παράξενον
  τοῦ φάνη,   45
διαγέρνη πρὸς τὸν Ἀυραὰμ καὶ ὅλα ταναθηβάνη.
Καβαλλικεύγει ὁ Ἀυραάμ, κεἰς τοὺς δαυλοὺς
  παγένη,
καὶ ὡς οἶδεν μετὰ μάτια του τὸ θαύμασμαν ποῦ
  γένη,
Ἐσίκοσεν τὰ χέρια του καὶ τὸν Θεὸν δοξάζει,
καὶ πλέον διακονοποίησιν τὸν Λὼτ οὐδὲν κο-
  πιάζη.   50
Τὸ ξύλον αὐτόνε ἡ λύτρωσις καὶ κάθαρσις ἁμαρ-
  τίας,
ἐλπίδα καὶ ἀπαντοχὴ τοῦ κόσμου σωτηρίας.
Ἡ ῥίζες του μὲ τὲς κορφές, εἰς τρία τὰ μοιράζη,
κ᾽ ἡ μέσες ἔνε κολλητές, ἔναν κορμὴν ὁμιάζη.
Καὶ ὡς εἶδεν ὁ Ἀυραὰμ τ᾽ ἁμάρτημαν καὶ αὐτὴν
  τὴν ἀσωτία,   55
καὶ ὁ Θεὸς ἐσυμπάθησεν, πάγει στὴν κατοικία.

XII. JOSEPH SOLD TO THE ISHMAELITES.
HE THROWS HIMSELF ON HIS MOTHER
RACHEL'S TOMB (Figs. 24, 25).

So comforting their selfish hearts to eat and drink
they sit:
  Joseph all starving and unclad they leave within
  the pit.
Lo! from afar a company with camels they did
see,
  Those camels heavy-laden were with myrrh and
  spicery.
That band from Ishmael's name was called, and
towards Egypt fares,   5
  For in that land they purpose hold to traffick
  with their wares.
No sooner did the brethren ten those traffickers
espy,
  Hoping they might their brother sell to them
  they did draw nigh.
On price of thirty silver coins they quickly did
agree,
  And for that sum their mother's son they sold
  to slavery.   10
They took those thirty silver coins—thus was
the bargain made,
  They gave their brother up, but then began to
  be afraid.
So they the travellers did approach, told them a
lying tale,
  Adding thereto full many an oath that it might
  more prevail.

XII

Λοιπὸν ἐφάγαν κ' οἴπγιασιν, καὶ ὅλοι θαραπαυτίκα,
τὸν Ἰωσὴφ ὁλόγδυμνον καὶ νηστικὸν ἐφήκαν.
Καὶ ἀπὸ μακριᾶς ἐνλέπουσιν καμίλια φορτομένα,
πολλὲς λογιὲς ἀρώματα ἦσαν σαυτὰ βαλμένα.
Κ' εἰσμαηλίταις τὰ λαλοῦν, κεῖναι πραματευτάδες,
στὴν Αἴγυπτον τα πιέννουσιν αὐτοίνοι οἱ
ὁμάδες.   6
Τὸ νὰ τοὺς δοῦν οἱ ἀδελφοί, τρέχουσι νὰ μιλήσουν,
νὰ κάμουσι τὴν συνείβασιν τ' ἀδέρφιν νὰ
πουλίσουν.
Ἀργύρια τριάκοντα ἀμάδιν συμφωνοῦσιν,
τὸν ἀδελφὸν τὸν ἴδιον ἄνομα τὸν πουλοῦσιν. 10
Καὶ πέρνουν τὰ ἀργύρια τὰ πιὰ συνηβαστίκα,
τὸν ἀδελφόν τους δίδουσιν, κεἰς μιὸν ἀπογνι-
αστίκα.
Κ' ὕστερα αὐτοὶ οἱ ἀδελφοὶ τοὺς ὁδοιπόρους λέγουν
μὲ ὅρκον συντυχένουν τους, ψόματα τοὺς ὁμνε-
γουν.

'Travellers,' said they, 'beware that lad for he is
    full of guiles,   15
  Guard him right carefully lest he deceive you
    with his wiles.'
Now for a moment let us leave Joseph in his distress,
  And turn to Jacob, on whom too did fall that
    wickedness.
The brothers slew a goat, and in its blood that
    coat did dip
  Of Joseph; then the coat they tore into full
    many a strip.   20
Thus torn they send it to their sire, tell him how
    it was found;
  They know not who its owner is, only their
    fears propound.
When Jacob saw that tattered coat, he knew it all
    too well,
  In anguish he did tear his beard—it was his
    son's death-knell.
  He rent his clothes, he rent his hair, and thus
    his grief did tell.   25
'O son for whom my heart doth yearn, O prey of
    fortune's spite,
  How couldst thou leave me, O my child, to
    this my hapless plight?
With that torn coat of thine, my son, to death
    I will descend,
  That there once more together knit my soul
    with thine may blend.'
Now let us turn our thoughts again to Joseph and
    his woe,   30
  Sold by his brethren false that he to slavery
    might go.

Πραματευτάδες, ξεύρεται, λέγομέ σας τὴν αἰτιάν
    του, 15

στὰ μάτια πιδεξεύεται μὴ πάγη τὴν δουλιάν του.

Τόρα λοιπὸν ἀς φήσωμεν τὸν Ἰωσὴφ τὸν ξένον
στὸν Ἰακὼβ νὰ δηγηθῶ τὸν παραπονημένον.

Τραγόπουλον ἐσφάξασι, τὸ αἷμαν περιεχήσαν
στοῦ Ἰωσὴφ ποκάμισο, καὶ τότες τὸ ξεσκίσα. 20

Τοῦ Ἰακὼβ τὸ πέμπουσι, λέγουν του πῶς τὸ
    υρίκαν,
καὶ αὐτὸν παραγνωρίζουσιν, κἔχουν μεγάλην
    προῖκαν.

Τὸ νὰ τὸ εἰδῆ ὁ Ἰακώβ, καθάρια τὸ γνωρίζη,
τὰ γένια του ἀνάσπασεν, καὶ μυριολόγια ἀρχίζει.

Τὰ ροῦχα του ἐξέσκισεν καὶ τὰ μαλιά του εὐγάνη
λυπητερά, φαρμακερά· ἄκω τί ἀναθηβάνη. 26

Τέκνον μου ποθεινότατον κὴ τύχει, τί μου πίκες ;
καὶ σὺ γλυκότατέ μου υἱέ, ἐμέναν ποῦ μ' ἀφίκες ;

Μὲ τὸ ποκάμισόν σου, υἱέ, νὰ κατευῶ στὸν Ἅδην,
γιὰ νὰ σμικτὴ ψυχήτζα μου με τὴν δική σου
    ὁμάδι. 30

Τόρα λοιπὸν ἀς διαγύρομεν στοῦ Ἰωσὴφ τοῦ
    ξένου,
τὸν 'παράδοκαν οἱ ἀδελφοὶ τοῦ παραπονεμένου.

Taking their captive in close guard, forth set those
    Ishmaelites,
  To whom a brother was betrayed by those cruel
    Israelites.
As Joseph went upon his way there came a tomb
    in sight,
  It was his mother Rachel's tomb as I above
    did write.   35
He ran unto that tomb and with sharp cries he
    filled the air,
  He kissed and clasped it in his arms and crying
    tore his hair.
'O mother Rachel, best beloved, enfold me to thy
    breast
  Here in this tomb where thou dost lie and
    takest thy long rest.'
Upon the sepulchre he fell and on his face he
    lay,   40
  And in his ecstasy of grief well nigh did swoon
    away.
When him upon that tomb outstretched the
    Ishmaelites did see,
  They thought he practised magic arts or some
    foul witchery,
That therewithal he might deprive them of their
    silver gain:
  They all rushed on him hoping thus their prize
    they might retain.   45
But as they nigh unto him drew, they found him
    as though dead,
  All over that angelic face a veil of tears was
    spread.

Ἐπίραν το, μισεύουσιν αὐτοίνοι Εἰσμαηλίταις,

καθὼς τὸν ἐπαράδωκαν αὐτοίνοι Ἰσραηλίταις.

Περνόντας υλέπη ἀπὸ μακρὰ τῆς Ραχιὴλ τὸν τάφον,

ὁποῦτον ἡ μητέρα του, ὡσὰν ἀπάνω γράφω.   36

Καὶ πρὸς τὸν τάφον ἔδραμεν, καὶ κλέει καὶ ἀνα-
καλιέτε,

φιλή, περιλαμπάνη τον, τότε σιρομαδιέτε.

Ὢ Ραχιήλ, μητέρα μου πολλά μου ἀγαπημένη,

δέξαι κ' ἐμὲν στὲς ἀγκάλες σου, αὐτοῦ ποῦσε
θαμένη.   40

Στὸν τάφον αὐτόνον πίκουππα ἔπεσεν ξαπλομένος,

καὶ ἀπὸ τὴν λύπην τὴν πολλὴν ἦτονε λλιγομένος.

Κ'εἰσμαηλίτες υλέποντας στὸν τάφον πῶς ξαπλόνη,

νομίζουν κατεργάζεται μαγίες, τοὺς κομπόνη.

Τὰ διάβη ὅπου νούλεται τὰ στάμενα νὰ χάσουν,   45

ὅλοι σ' αὐτὸν ἐδράμασιν νὰ πᾶν νὰ τὸν ἐπιάσουν.

Καὶ ἀπίτης τοῦ σιμόσασιν, βρίσκουν τον λλιγο-
μένον,

τὸ πρόσωπον τ' ἀγγελικὸν τὰ δάκρυα φορτο-
μένον.

M   7

So at the sight of that great grief they too to
  weeping fell;
 Those herdsmen wrongfully (they thought) did
  him to slavery sell.
They asked him who his father was and where his
  home did lie,   50
 What chance had brought him to that pit,
  abandoned there to die.
Whether he was the herdsmen's slave and food
  from them had got,
 Or whether he a freeman was who had been
  ta'en by plot.
'To look upon thy comely face an angel might'st
  thou be,
 How was it that thou fell'st among such evil
  company?'   55
And to their words he answer made: 'Never was
  I a slave,
 But I went forth because to me my sire com-
  mandment gave
That I should seek my brethren out—they are
  the men ye saw,
 Those herdsmen are my father's sons and blood
  from his veins draw.
The sepulchre that ye behold—that is my mother's
  grave;   60
 Before my very eyes my sire burial to her there
  gave.'
Then spake one of those Hagarenes, listen to what
  he said:
 He bade the boy be of good cheer and tears no
  more to shed.

Στοχάζουντε τὴν λύπην του, καὶ ὅλοι τους ἐδα-
    κριόσα,
λογιάζουσιν πῶς οἱ νοσκοὶ ἄδικα τὸν πολίσαν.
Ροτούν τον τίνος ἦτονε, καὶ πόθεν ἐνεφάνη,   51
    κ' ἡ τύχη πῶς τὸν ἤφερεν στὸν λάκκον νὰ
    ποθάνη.
Εἶαν ἦτον δοῦλος τῶν βοσκῶν, καὶ αὐτοὶ τὸν
    ἐνεθρέψα,
ἢ πάλιν ἂν ἦτον λεύτερος, καὶ κεῖνοι τὸν ἐκλέψα.
Καὶ ἀκ τὴν θεωριάν σου φένεσε μᾶς ἄγγελος στὴν
    θεωρία,   55
    μὰ πῶς ἐσὺ συγκλήθηκες με τ' ἄγρια τὰ θηρία;
Καὶ αὐτὸς ἐπηλογήθηκεν, ποτὲ δοῦλος δὲν ἤμουν,
    παραγγελιὰν ἐπάκουσα νὰ κάμω τοῦ γονῆ μου.
Σ' αὐτοὺς τοὺς λέγεται βοσκοὺς παιδιάνε τοῦ
    κυρού μου,
    καὶ μέναν ἴνε ἀδέλφια μου, τὸ πάθαέτυρού μου.
Τὸ μνῆμαν ὁποῦ υλέπετε αὐτόνε τῆς μητρός μου,   61
    καὶ 'Ιακὼβ ὁ κύρις μου αὐτὴν ἔθαψεν ὀμπρός
    μου.
Καὶ εἷς ἀπὸ τοὺς 'Αγαρηνούς, ἄκου τὸ τί τοῦ λέγει,
    παρηγορὰ τὸν νέον αὐτόν, μὴδὲ ποσὸς νὰ κλέγει.

'Nay, be not over-much cast down, be brave,
    good heart, not sad,
    In Egypt thou wilt lead the life of some great
    prince's lad.'   65

XIII. BIRTH OF MOSES. HIS ORDEAL BEFORE PHARAOH (Figs. 26, 27).

But in due time God purpose had that race enslaved
    to free,
    And Israel from its heavy yoke to set at
    liberty.
'Twas then a babe was born, and smiles did
    wreathe his comely face;
    Moses the name they gave to him, he was a
    child of grace.
No cries were from his cradle heard, as is an
    infant's way,   5
    He crowed and bubbled o'er with mirth, at all
    times seemed he gay.
By grace divine he destined was Pharaoh to over-
    throw
    With all that monarch's band, and free his people
    by this blow.
For him his parents built an ark and launched it in
    the Nile,
    They set that babe within the ark, and still his
    face did smile.   10
That ark well caulked with pitch was launched upon
    the very day
    When Pharaoh's daughter for pastime on the
    river's bank did stray.

Μὴ δὲν κακοκαρδῆς πολλά, ὡς νέον παλλικαράκιν,
στὴν Αἴγυπτον διὰ να θραφῇς ὡς ἀφεντὸς
παιδάκιν. 66

XIII

Καὶ ὡσὰν ἐθέλησεν ὁ Θεὸς τὸ γένος νὰ λυτρώσει,
τὸν Ἰσραὴλ ἐκ τὴν σκλαβιὰν αὐτούνους νὰ
λαφρόσι,
Ἕναν παιδὶν ἐγενήθηκεν, πολλὰ τὸν γελατζάρη,
Μωσῆς ἐπονομάστικεν, κεῖχεν περίσσα χάριν.
Δὲν ἔκλεγεν ὡς νήπιον, ὡσὰν τὸ θέλη τάξη, 5
μὰ γέλαν καὶ χαχάνιζεν, ἤμελλεν κατὰ τάξιν
Τὸν Φαραὼ μὲ τοὺς ἄρχοντες καὶ συντροφιὰν
μεγάλην
διὰ τὸν λαὸν τοῦ Ἰσραὴλ τὸν ἤμελεν ναυγάλη.
Τὸ λοιπὸν ἡ γονέη του βάνουν το σε κασέλα,
καλαφατίζουν, φτιάνουν την, καὶ αὐτοῦνος μέσα
γέλα. 10
Καὶ ρίκτουν τον στὸν ποταμὸν ἐκείνην τὴν ἡμέραν
τοῦ Φαραὼ εἰς ξιφάντωσιν ἐδιάβη θυγατέρα.

And as she went down to the shore with her
    attendant band,
  She saw the ark, and eagerly she drew it to the
    strand.
With her own hands she raised the lid and looked
    upon the child;   15
  Lo! there a babe slept peacefully, and through
    its tears it smiled.
That sight so strange within her mind did a great
    wonder wake,
  She would (said she) from out the ark the sleep-
    ing Moses take.
That Hebrew name doth signify 'from out the
    water drawn,'
  But in the Egyptian tongue it means 'a child to
    blessing born.'   20
That infant did the Princess take as though he
    were her son,
  And as an only child beloved wealth's lavishment
    he won.
The mark of circumcision showed he was a Hebrew
    boy,
  She hid him from her sire lest he his wrath
    'gainst him employ.
His mother's sister saw the child (Maria was her
    name),   25
  And knowing who the infant was, she to the
    Princess came,
And said: 'Great lady, let me find for thee a
    faithful dame
  From whom that child may nurse's skill and
    fond attention claim.'

Καὶ κατεβένει στὸν γιαλὸν μὲ συντροφιὰ μεγάλην,
καὶ τ᾽ ὅρμημαν τοῦ ποταμοῦ αὐτῆ θέλει ναυγάλη.
Καὶ μετὰ χέρια της ἔπιασεν κἔνοιξεν τὴν κασέλα,
καὶ τὸ παιδάκην ἐρήνευε, σὰν τίς νὰ κλέγει,
ἐγέλα.   16
Καὶ ὡς εἶδεν τὸ παράξενον θαύμασμαν τὸ μεγάλον,
λέγει πρὸς τὲς ἀρχόντισσες Μωσὴν νὰ τὸν
εὐγάλω.
Τ᾽ ὄνομαν ξεδιαλύνετε ἐκ τὰ νερὰ βαλμένος,
στὴν γλῶσσαν τὴν αἰγυπτιακὴν μάτον εὐλογη-
μένος.   20
Καὶ αὐτίνη τὸν παράλαβεν υἱόν της ἀγαπημένον,
καὶ μὲ παράταξες πολλὲς τὸν εἶχεν υλεπημένον.
Καὶ ἀπὸ τὸ περιτόμημαν ὀβριόπουλλον ἐφάνη,
χόνη τον διὰ τὸν Φαραώ, ὀγιὰ νὰ μὴν ἀποθάνη.
Ἡ θία τοῦ Μωϋσῆ, τὴν λέγουσιν Μαρία,   25
τὰνίψιν της ἐγνώρισεν, ζητά της ἐγγαρία.
Καιρά, βασιλοπούλα μου, νὰ σού βρω ἐγὼ βιζά-
στρια,
νὰποκρατίση τὸ παιδὶν μὲ τὴν μεγάλην σπάστρα.

The Princess answered: 'Let it be, money I do
    not spare;
  The task I give into thy hands, the payment is
    my care.'   30
She sought the mother of the boy, and her she
    made his nurse,
  And for that charge the Princess did a royal fee
    disburse.
The infant Moses at four years they to the Princess
    bring,
  With joy she took him in her arms, dear as her
    own offspring.
She clasped him close unto her breast, with wealth
    of kisses dowered,   35
  On lips and forehead and on cheeks were they in
    plenty showered.
She carried him within the hall that he her lord
    might greet,
  Just as king Pharaoh sat him down at table to
    take meat.
Full kindly Pharaoh welcomed him and in his arms
    upbore;
  The boy stretched out his hands, and lo! the
    monarch's beard he tore!   40
The king was seized with anger fierce, and bade his
    thralls remove
  The infant Moses out of sight, lest he a danger
    prove,
And take from him the breath of life: 'For this
    wide Egypt's realm
  (So from such conduct I presage) he's destined
    to o'erwhelm.'

Καὶ λέγει της ἡ βασίλεισσα, μὴ λυπηθὴς δυνάρια,
ὀμπρὸς δίδω τὸ πλέρομαν εἰς τὰ δικά της
χέρια.   30
Βρίσκη τὴν μάναν τοῦ παιδιοῦ, σαυτὴν τὸ παρα-
δόκαν,
ξένια πολλὰ καὶ στάμενα στὰ χέρια της τὰ
δόκαν.
Χρόνῶν τεσσάρων γίνεται, στὴν δέσποιναν τὸ
φέρνει,
μὲ τὴν χαρὰν τὸ δέκτικεν, γιὰ υἱόν της τὸν
ἐπέρνη.
Σφύγγει, περιλαμπάνη τον, γλυκιὰ τὸ καταφίλει,
στὰ μάγουλα, στὸ κούτελλον, στὸ στόμαν κ' εἰς
τὰ χείλει.   36
Σικόνη τον στὰ χέρια της, στὸν βασιλέα τὸν πάγη,
ὄντανέκατζεν ὁ Φαραὼς στὴν τράπεζαν νὰ φάγη.
Ὁ Φαραὼς τὸν ἐφιλῆ, καὶ ὀμπρός του τὸν ἐβάνη,
καὶ τὸ παιδάκιν ἤπλωσεν τὰ γένια του ναυγάλη.
Θυμώνεται ὁ Φαραώς, θέλει νὰ καταλύση   41
αὐτῶ τὸ υρέφος τὸν Μωσῆν, θέλη νὰ ναφανήσει.
Εἶπεν εἰς παρατήρημαν, μέλλει νὰ ναφανίσει
τὴν βασιλιὰν καὶ τὸν λαὸν νὰ μοῦ καταποντίση.

'Nay,' said his daughter unto him, 'this passion to
    display   45
  Against a child is all unjust, 'tis but an infant's
    way.
But that thou mayest see by trial he knew not
    what he did,
  A testing for his infant mind I thee to frame
    would bid.
In two twin bowls bright coins and fire I'd have
    thee set to view :
  If the child hankers for the coins—then will thy
    charge be true.'   50
So forthwith Pharaoh gave command, and fire and
    coins they set,
  Straightway the babe did lift the fire till it and
    his lips met.
The flames that flicker on his tongue his utterance
    impair ;
  The bitterness of pain was such that he did tear
    his hair.
So Pharaoh comfort had about the plucking of his
    beard,   55
  Moses had done it without spite and was not to
    be feared.

XIV. DEATH OF MOSES AND HIS BURIAL ON SINAI (Fig. 28).

He gave command : in Sinai's soil they dug a grave
    so laid
  As to befit his frame ; thereof Moses a trial
    made.

Λέγει του ἡ θυγατέρα του, μὴν ὀργιστὴς τὸ
    υρέφος,   45
δέν τό καμεν ὀγια κακόν, αὐτοῦνον τὰναθρέφω.

Μὰ θὲν νὰ δῆς τὴν γνῶσιν σου, ἀνεγροικὰ στὰ
    κάμνη,
    δοκίμασέ τον ἠς τὸ σου πῶ, εἰς μιὸν νὰ δῆς
    ἀσφάλλη.

Βάλεσε δύο κατατομαῖς, δουκάτα καὶ φωτία,
    καὶ ἀλυμπιστὴ τὰ στάμενα, δικαιώνι σε ἡ
    αἰτία.   50

Ὁρίζῃ, φέρνουσιν φωτιά, καὶ στάμενα τοῦ πιάνη,
    τὸ υρέφος πιάνη τὴν φωτιά, στὸ στόμαν του
    τὴν βάνη.

Καὶ κάγικεν ἡ γλῶσσα του, χάννεται ἡ ἐμιλιά του,
    καὶ ἀπὲ τὸν πόνον τὸν πολὺν ἔσυρνεν τὰ μαλιά
    του.

Κ' εἰς μιὸν νομίζει ὁ βασιλεὺς γιάπλωσις τῶν
    γενιῶν του,   55
    ἀπαγνωσιάν του ὁ Μωϋσῆς τὴν ἔκαμεν στανιό
    του.

XIV

Ὁρίζῃ, κάτω σκάφτουσι πρὸς τὸ Σινὰ τὸ ὄρει
εἰς ὅσον ἤτονε σοστόν, καὶ ὁ Μωϋσῆς ἐχώρη.

He entered it as though to test if it were made
    aright,
  And straight the Lord sent down a mist and hid
    him out of sight.
So veiled from out his people's eyes Moses was
    lost to view ;   5
  Great fear upon them fell and all into amaze-
    ment threw.

Ἐμπένη μέσα ὁ Μωϋσῆς σαύτον νὰ δικημάσι,
καὶ ὁ Κύριος πέμπει νέφαλον αὐτοῦνον νὰ
σκεπάσι.

Λοιπὸν αὐτὸν ἐσκέπασεν, καὶ ὁ Μωϋσῆς ἐχάθη, 5
καὶ ἀπὸ τὸν φόβον ὁ λαὸς ὅλος ἐπαραπάρθη.

NOTES ON THE GREEK TEXT

I 14. περιπατοῦν στὸ γόν τος. Probably means 'walk by themselves.' τὸ γόν τος seems to stand for τὸ γώ τους. Elsewhere in the poem τὸ γώ σας occurs with the meaning 'yourselves.'

18. κοντεύγοντας τὰ γόνατα. Seems to mean 'shortening their knees,' i.e. 'falling on their knees.' Cf. Xanthoudides, *Eritocritos*, *Glossary*, *s.v.* κοντεύγομαι.

II 4. ἡ γῆς ἔνε τοῦ μόδου του. Probably means 'the earth is at his disposal.' Xanthoudides, *op. cit.*, notes the use of μόδος in Crete=τρόπος, e.g. εἶναι τοῦ μόδου ντου=ἰδιότροπος.

15. σεσὲν νὰ μένε τάξη. Probably 'an arrangement (or promise) will remain for thee.'

III 5. ἔξεν=ἔζη? 'His skill lived with hunting' i.e. 'all his skill was devoted to hunting.'

12. διαβλογητικές του = διὰ εὐλογητικάς του 'for his married wives.'

20. ναπλικέψη. Uncertain. Apparently from ἀπλικένω 'I dwell.' Prof. Dawkins suggests a connection with Lat. *applicare*.

29. ἤτια=τέτοια (τοιαῦτα). See *Glossary*. Frequently occurs in the poem.

IV 56. σταδά. Perhaps connected with ἐδά or δά 'now.' See Xanthoudides, *Glossary*. 'The sword which now has entered my heart like a nail.'

72. στὸ καλάμιν. 'In the reeds.'

102. ἐν κεντρώση. So MS. κεντρόνω means 'I graft,' but (δ) has probably fallen out, and the sense is 'will not graft the roots together.'

VII 47. τίσονε. Apparently for τίς σοῦ εἶνε.

50. ἐμπασάν. Apparently for ἔμβασιν or ἐμβασιάν: 'Whence dost thou make journey into Palestine?'

VIII 60. ἀπόλωνα. I feel doubtful as to the interpretation. If it ='Απόλ(λ)ωνα, then the meaning will be 'to sacrifice me to his gods, even to Apollo.'

80. I cannot explain the line. ἐντηρούμου appears to be connected with ἐντηροῦμαι=φοβοῦμαι. Cf. Xanthoudides, *Glossary*, *s.v.* ἐντήρησι.

IX 27. σιμηδόλαδον. Lit. 'flour and oil.'

44. ὅδελέγοντας. I cannot explain. Can there be any connection with ὁ διαλεγῶνας = ἐκλογή (Xanthoudides, *Glossary*)?

X 10. πιένετε ἀνάθεμά σας. 'Go to the devil.'

19. δυναμάρη. Lit. 'fortress.'

40. μεστίαν ἀντουμένην = μ' ἐστίαν ἁφτομένην. ἅφτω = 'I kindle.'

50. καναβιτζένη. καννάβι = 'hemp.'

XI 9. ἐξεξήνησεν…τὸ φορέθην. Apparently means 'Recovered from the maze into which he had been put.'

37. αὐτοῦνον ὡς τακοῦσι. Uncertain. ?'As they listen to him.'

38. νἀθθίσουν = νὰ ἀνθίζουν.

XII 5. τὰ λαλοῦν. Perhaps 'drive them' (ἐλαύνω).

60. τὸ πάθαέτυρού μου. Doubtful. ?'I suffered it from my comrade.'

XIII 26. ἐγγαρία. ? = ἀγγαρία 'service.'

27. καιρά = κερά. 'Mistress,' 'lady.'

29. μὴ λυπηθὴς δυνάρια. 'Do not trouble about money.' δυνάρια = δηνάρια.

43. εἰς παρατήρημαν. ?'On observing it.'

48. ἀσφάλλη = ἂν σφάλλη. 'If he is in the wrong.' Cf. xiii. 50, ἀλυμπιστή = ἂν λυμπιστή : iv. 80, ἀδῆς = ἂν ἰδῆς.

GLOSSARY

NOTE. By far the most useful collection of words for the interpretation of Chumnos's poem will be found in Xanthoudides' *Glossary* to his edition of Kornaros' *Erotocritos* (Candia, 1915). I have also found E. Brighenti's *Dizionario Greco-Moderno* of great use.

In the present select *Glossary* I have tried to include such words as would be most likely to cause difficulty to a reader who is acquainted with Ancient but not with Modern Greek. The references are to the number and line of the selections. As a rule the first passage only in which the word occurs is given. I have not adhered to the phonetic spelling of the MS., but have given the ordinarily received form of the words.

'Αγκαλά, VI 41, *although*
ἀγροικῶ, III 31, *perceive*
ἀθῶ (ἀνθίζω), XI 38, *blossom*
ἀκατωμένος (ἀνακατόνω), X 39, *mixed, embroiled*
ἀκκουμπίζω, III 15, *lean*
ἀλλήλως, I 35, *together*
ἄλλης λοῆς, VII 78, *of another sort.* Cf. πᾶσα λοῆς, *of every sort*
ἄμαν, VIII 27, *please*
ἀμέ, VIII 40, *but*
ἀμέτε, II 33, *bear, carry*
ἀναγυρίζω, VII 94, *turn*
ἀναθηβάνω, IV 23, *speak, tell*
ἀναπαύγω, VII 69, *rest*
ἀνέν, VII 13, *even if, though*
ἀντρανίζω (ἀνεντρανίζω), VIII 89, *look*
ἀπαντοχή, XI 52, *hope, expectation*
ἀπήτις, VII 31, *after, when*
ἀπολογιάζω, ἀπιλογοῦμαι, II 3, *answer*
ἀποσυντυχαίνω, VIII 103, *converse*
ἀπού, ἀπέ (ἀπό), VI 43, *from*
ἀσβολόνω, X 15, *smoke, burn*
ἄσπρος, IV 66, *white*
αὐγίτζα, VIII 45, *break of day*
ἀφεντεύω, VIII 48, *rule*

ἀφέντης, X 20, *lord, master*
ἀφίνω, VII 2, *leave*

Βάνω, I 22, *put*
βαραανασττενάζω, II 28, *sigh heavily*
βαριοῦμαι, IV 30, *grow weary of*
βασιλεύω, I 16, *set (sun)*
βορκόνω, IV 24, *swell with tears*
βοσκός, II 3, *shepherd*
βο(υ)λάω, X 43, *overwhelm*
βουλησ(ι)ά, X 38, *overthrow, submerging*
βουνός, βουνί, βουνόν, II 10, *mountain*
βράδι, VII 29, *evening*
βυζάνω, IV 86, *suckle*
βυζάστρ(ι)α, XIII 27, *nurse*
βυθίζω, VIII 94, *submerge*

Γδίνω, VII 30, *strip*
γεμόζω, VIII 58, *fill*
γέρος, VI 57, *old, old man*
γιαγέρνω (διαγέρνω), IV 78, *turn*
γιαλός, XIII 13, *shore*
γλήγορα, IX 23, *quickly*
γλυτόνω, VII 13, *save, escape*
γνεύω, X 4, *make a sign*
γυρεύω, VII 50, *seek*

Δείχνω, IX 15, *seem*
δέννω, IX 19, *tie, interlace*
δέρνομαι, II 28, *lament*
διαβάζω, VIII 35, *pass* (not *read*)
δοκάρι, VII 35, *beam*
δοξεύγω, III 3, *shoot with bow*
δυναμάρι, X 19, *fortress*
δυνάριον, XIII 29, *money*

Εβγάζω, ἐβγάνω, I 33, *put out,
lead*
ἐβγαίνω, I 28, *go out*
ἐγγαρία (ἀγγαρία), XIII 26, *task,
service*
ἐγγαστρόνω (γαστρώνομαι), XI 8,
make pregnant, become pregnant
ἐγδημία, VIII 32, *exile*
ἐδικός, ἰδικός II 4, *own*
εἰς μιόν, I 21, *suddenly*
ἐλικιά, IV 7, *stature*
ἐμιλιά, XIII 53, *speech*
ἐντηροῦμαι, VIII 80 (?), *fear*
ἐντροπιάζω, VII 42, *shame*
ἐπιλογίζομαι, II 3, *reply*
ἐρμοχάρακον, XI 30, *barren rock*
ἔτιος, ἤτιος, III 29, *such*
εὔκαιρος, VI 52, *vain*

Ζυγόνω, II 11, *expel, drive out*
ζωντόβολον, VII 78, *beast*

Ητιος, see ἔτιος

Θέ, θές, III 39 = θέλει, θέλεις
θωρῶ, IV 89, *see*

Καιρά (κυρία), XIII 27, *lady*
καλά καί, IV 30, *although*
καλαφατίζω, XIII 10, *caulk*
καλύβη, IX 25, *tent, hut*
κάμνω, IV 35, *do, make*
καναβιτζένη, X 50, *hemp*
κανένας, VII 4, (*no*) *one*
κασέλα, XIII 9, *box, ark*
κατὰ πῶς, IV 121, *as*
κατανταω, VII 61, *arrive*
κατατομή, XIII 49, *section, division*
κείτομαι, IV 90, *lie*
κεντρόνω, IV 102, *graft*

κομπόνω, XII 44, *bewitch* (literally
'*tie*')
κοντά, IV 74, *near*
κοπέλι, III 7, *boy*
κορμί, II 14, *body*
κορφή, IV 85, *top*
κουβαλῶ, XI 36, *bring, transport*
κουράζω, VI 61, *tire*
κουρεύω, VIII 25, *cut hair*
κουρφά, VII 52, *secretly*
κούτελλον, XIII 36, *forehead*
κρασί, VIII 3, *wine*
κρημνίζω (γκρεμνίζω), VIII 93,
throw headlong
κροῦσμα, III 31, *noise, sound*
κύρης, III 35, *father*

Λαγκαδάκι, X 36, *little vale*
λάδι, IV 28, *oil*
λαφρόνω, XIII 2, *relieve*
λεύτερος (ἐλεύθερος), XII 54, *free*
λέω, IX 31, *say*
λιγένω, IV 131, *grow less*
λιγόνομαι, XII 42, *faint*
λιξεύω, X 3, *lust*
λόγου μου, σου, IV 27, *myself, thyself*
λυμιόνα, III 22, *devastator*
λυμπίζομαι, XIII 50, *desire eagerly*

Μάγουλον, XIII 36, *cheek*
μαδῶ, μαδίζω, IV 76, *strip of leaves*
μαζόνω, VIII 71, *collect*
μαλαία, VIII 65, *strife, anger*
μαλλί, VIII 8, *hair*
μάνιτα, VIII 58, *frenzy*
μάστορας, VI 14, *master workman*
μάτι, VIII 10, *eye*
μαῦρος, II 20, *black*
μισεύω, I 13, *set out*
μνέγω, VII 38, *swear*
μονοπάτι, X 35, *path*
μπορετός, IV 38, *possible*
(μ)πορῶ, X 21, *can, be able*
μυρ(ι)ολόγιον, XII 24, *funeral
lament*

Νάνε (νὰ εἶναι), IV 29
νερό, IV 66, *water*

Ξαπλόνω, XII 41, *stretch out*
ξαστερωμένα, VIII 45, *clear (sky)*
ξεξενίζω, XI 9, *recover from wonder*
ξεπόλυτος, I 14, *unshod*
ξεύρω, XII 15, *know*
ξεφυτρόνω, IV 38, *grow*
ξεχωριστά, VII 70, *separately*
ξημερομένα, VIII 46, *break of day*
ξιφάντωσις, XIII 12, *pastime*

Ὀγιά, ὀδιά(= διά), IV 28
ὀμιλῶ, μιλῶ, IV 25, *speak*
ὀμορφιά, IV 134, *beauty*
ὀμπρός, ἐμπρός, II 6, *before*
ὄντας, ὄντες, ὄντεν, II 7, *when*
ὄρμημα, XIII 14, *rush*

Παίρνω, πέρνω, III 9, *take*
παλληκάρι, II 34, *brave young man*
πάντα, IV 34, *always*
παραπαίρνομαι, XIV 6, *to become distraught*
παραπονῶ, XII 32, *afflict*
παράταξις, XIII 22, *attention, nurture*
παρατήρημα, XIII 43, *observation, presage*
πγήστε (ποῖοι εἶστε), X 19, *who are ye?*
πειράζω, III 38, *trouble, annoy*
πεντίντα, IV 130, *fifty*
περιλαμπάνω, IV 24, *embrace*
περ(ι)μαζόνω, VI 46, *collect*
περ(ι)πατῶ, IV 43, *walk*
περιπλέκω, XI 38, *interlace*
περνῶ, II 25, *pass*
πετῶ (ἐπέταξα), II 14, *cast, throw*
πηγαίνω, VIII 28, *go*
πιδευξεύομαι, XII 16, *act with cleverness, do one's best*
πίκουππα, XII 41, *on the nose, on the face*
πλάγι, VII 33, *side*
πληρωμή, XIII 30, *payment*
πλουμίζω, IV 63, *adorn*
ποκάμισο, XII 20, *shirt*
πορίος, VII 9, *ripe* (?), (cf. πωρικός)

ποσῶς, III 39, *(not) at all*
πουλῶ, XII 8, *sell*
πρίκα (πικρία), IX 11, *bitterness, affliction*

Ρίκτω, XIII 11, *throw*
ρίφνητος, IV 82, *numberless*
ροῦχον, VIII 2, *garment*

Σάζω, III 7, *arrange*
σάν, ὡσάν, II 19, *like, as*
σηκόνω, I 13, *raise*
σημόνω, III 32, *approach*
σιμά, IV 71, *near*
σιμηδόλαδον, IX 27, *flour and oil*
σιρομαδίζω, XII 38, *tear the hair*
σκοτόνω, II 24, *kill*
σμίγω, XII 30, *join*
σομαρικόν (σαμάρι), VIII 1, *packsaddle*
σπάστρα (πάστρα), XIII 28, *cleanliness*
σπαστρικός (παστρικός), VIII 2, *clean*
σπειράκι, IV 100, *seed*
σπίτι, VI 42, *house*
στάμενα, XII 45, *money*
στανιό, III 34, *unwillingly*
στέκω, VIII 14, *stand*
στίνω, IX 3, *set*
στοχάζομαι, IV 81, *consider*
στράτα, IX 7, *street*
συμπαθῶ, XI 18, *pardon*
συντυχιά, II 1, *conversation*
σύρω, σύρνω, III 3, *draw*, passive, *creep*
σφαλίζω, I 6, *shut*
σφοντιλιά, III 33, *backbone, back*
σώνω, III 19, *arrive*
σωστός, XIV 2, *exact*

Τάσιμον, VIII 115, *promise*
τάσσω, VIII 111, *promise*
ταχύ, VII 72, *early morning*
τέρι, ταίρι, VII 54, *partner, husband, wife*
τέτοιος, VII 52, *such*
τίβοτες, VIII 70, *nothing*
τόρα, X 22, *now*

τριγυρίζω, IV 73, *surround*

Ὑπάγω, πάγω, πάω, II 2, *go*

Φασκιόνω, IV 85, *wrap in bands*
φεγγάρι, I 24, *moon*
φελῶ, IV 28, *benefit*
φλοῦδι, IV 75, *bark*
φόρος, VI 17, *market*
φουμίζω (εὐφημίζω), IV 104, *praise, celebrate*
φταίω (πταίω), X 16, *sin*

φτιάνω, XIII 10, *make*

Χάνω, I 17, *lose*
χαράκι, II 33, *rock*
χαχ(λ)ανίζω, XIII 6, *burst into laughter*
χρόνος, IV 115, *year*
χώνω, III 16, *insert, hide*

Ψόμα, ψέμα, IV 129, *lie*
ψωμί, VIII 3, *bread*

Fig. 1. Adam and Eve at the Cave of Nevron.

Fig. 2. Lamech, his son, and Cain.

Fig. 3. Adam, Eve, and Seth.

Fig. 4. Seth, the Archangel, and the Babe in Paradise.

Fig. 5. Seth returns from Paradise.

Fig. 6. The branches sprout from the mouth of the dead Adam.

Fig. 7. Enoch inscribes the Story of Creation on marble tablets.

Fig. 8. Terah makes idols for Abram to carry to market.

Fig. 9. Abram converted by beholding the wonders of the heavens.

Fig. 10. The journey to Mesopotamia.

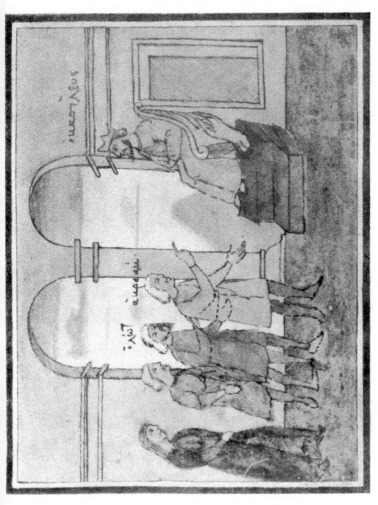

Fig. 11. Abraham, Lot and Sarah before the King of Canaan.

Fig. 12. The King of Canaan's banquet.

Fig. 13. The Angel prevents the King's designs on Sarah.

Fig. 14. Abraham arrives at Melchisedek's cave.

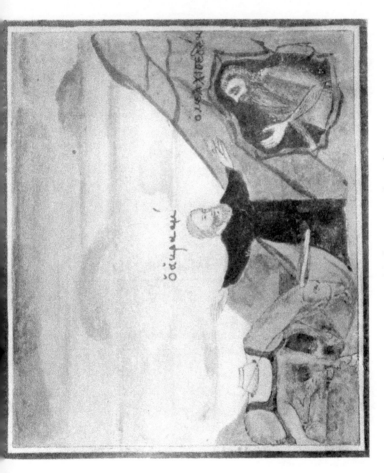

Fig. 15. Melchisedek emerges from the cave.

Fig. 16. Abraham shears Melchisedek.

Fig. 17. Melchisedek and the babes of the city of Salem.

Fig. 18. Abraham invites the three young travellers.

Fig. 19. The miracle of the resurrected calf.

Fig. 20. The assault on Lot's house.

Fig. 21. The miracle of the flame.

Fig. 22. Lot fetches the brands from the Nile.

Fig. 23. Abraham and Lot see the brands blossoming.

Fig. 24. Joseph sold to the Ishmaelites.

Fig. 25. Joseph throws himself upon Rachel's tomb.

Fig. 26. Moses pulls Pharaoh's beard.

Fig. 27. Moses submitted to the ordeal of fire and gold.

Fig. 28. Moses directs the making of his tomb.

For EU product safety concerns, contact us at Calle de José Abascal, 56–1°, 28003 Madrid, Spain or eugpsr@cambridge.org.

www.ingramcontent.com/pod-product-compliance
Ingram Content Group UK Ltd.
Pitfield, Milton Keynes, MK11 3LW, UK
UKHW012331130625
459647UK00009B/215